P9-AFW-541

Social Security

Social Security

A Critique of Radical Reform Proposals

Edited by
Charles W. Meyer
Iowa State University

Lexington Books
D.C. Heath and Company/Lexington, Massachusetts/Toronto

Library of Congress Cataloging-in-Publication Data

Social security

  Bibliography: p.
  Includes index.
  Contents: Social security / Charles W. Meyer —
Phasing out social security : a critique of Ferrara's
proposal / Bruno Stein — Intercohort and intracohort
redistribution under social security / Charles W. Meyer
and Nancy L. Wolff — [etc.]
  1. Social security—United States. I. Meyer,
Charles W.
HD7125.S593   1987   368.4'3'00973   86–45891
ISBN 0–669–14518–1 (alk. paper)

Published simultaneously in Canada
Printed in the United States of America
Casebound International Standard Book Number: 0–669–14518–1
Library of Congress Catalog Card Number: 86–45891

The paper used in this publication meets the minimum requirements of
American National Standard for Information Sciences—Permanence of
Paper for Printed Library Materials, ANSI Z39.48–1984. ∞™

87 88 89 90 91 8 7 6 5 4 3 2 1

Contents

Figures

Tables

Acknowledgments

The material in tables 3–1, 3–2, and 3–3 first appeared in Anthony Pellechio and Gordon Goodfellow, "Individual Gains and Losses from Social Security Before and After the 1938 Amendments," *Cato Journal,* Fall 1983, 3(2), pp. 436–438. It is reprinted with permission of the Cato Institute.

Chapter 4, "Social Security and Private Saving: Theory and Historical Evidence" by Selig D. Lesnoy and Dean R. Leimer, first appeared in the *Social Security Bulletin* (48), January 1985, pp. 15–30. It is reprinted with permission of the authors.

The editor wishes to thank Donna Otto for her assistance in preparing the manuscript.

Social Security

1
Social Security: Past, Present, and Future

Charles W. Meyer

The Origin and Evolution of Social Security

Extensive social insurance programs are found in many nations, including all of the advanced market-oriented industrial nations. Programs differ widely in means of finance and in benefit structure. Some are financed out of general tax revenues; others are supported by earmarked taxes on earnings. Monthly benefits may be a fixed amount for all recipients or may vary according to past taxable earnings. Rights to benefit payments are typically derived from prior labor force attachments. Workers and their families are insured against loss of income owing to retirement, disability, and unemployment. In many countries the cost of medical care is covered by public insurance or a national health service.

Overview of Social Security

The cornerstone of the American system of social insurance is the old age, survivors, disability and hospital insurance program, or OASDHI. This portion of the Social Security system is financed by a payroll tax shared equally by employees and employers and by a tax on the earnings of the self-employed. Tax receipts are allocated among three separate trust funds: old age and survivors insurance (OASI), disability insurance (DI), and hospital insurance (HI).

The tax on earnings is applied at a flat rate to earnings of all workers in covered occupations. The currently legislated tax rates shown in table 1–1 were set by the 1983 Social Security Amendments.

The rates apply to earnings up to the annual taxable ceiling. The ceiling, which stood at $42,000 in 1986, is adjusted upward automatically each year at a rate equal to the annual percentage increase in average wages. Ceilings through 1990, as projected by Social Security Administration actuaries, along with the projected maximum tax contribution, appear in table 1–2.

The OASDHI trust funds operate on a pay-as-you-go basis. Payments to

Table 1–1

Old Age and Survivors, Disability, and Hospital Insurance Tax Rates[a]

	Employer and Employee (percent)				Combined	Self-employed			
	OASI	DI	HI	OASDHI	OASDHI	OASI	DI	HI	OASDHI[b]
1986–87	5.2	0.5	1.45	7.15	14.3	10.4	1.0	2.9	14.3
1988–89	5.53	0.53	1.45	7.51	15.02	11.06	1.06	2.9	15.02
1990–99	5.6	0.6	1.45	7.65	15.3	11.2	1.2	2.9	15.3
2000 and later	5.49	0.71	1.45	7.65	15.3	10.98	1.42	2.9	15.3

[a] Rates under legislation in effect Jan. 1, 1986

[b] Effective rates on self-employed are reduced by tax credits of 2 percent in 1986–89.

Table 1–2

Contribution Base and Maximum Tax Contribution per Worker, 1986–90

Year	Tax Rate, Employer, and Employee Combined (percent)	Contribution Base[a]	Maximum Tax Contribution
1986	14.3	$42,000	$6,006
1987	14.3	43,500	6,220
1988	15.02	45,300	6,804
1989	15.02	47,700	7,165
1990	15.3	50,100	7,665

Source: U.S. Congress, Committee on Ways and Means (1986b), p. 114.

[a] Base for 1987 through 1990 is the intermediate IIB estimate of Social Security Administration Actuaries.

the more than 36 million beneficiaries are financed mainly from current payroll tax collections. Trust fund balances are invested in U.S. government securities, but interest income is minimal because fund balances are large enough to cover only a few months' benefit payments.

Old Age and Survivors Insurance (OASI). The old-age and survivors insurance program (OASI) is by far the largest component of the Social Security system, accounting for 80 percent of OASDHI disbursements. Beneficiaries include retired workers and dependents, along with surviving dependents of deceased workers.

Workers become eligible for full benefits at age 65. They may apply for reduced benefits as early as age 62 or receive incremental benefits for delayed retirement after age 65. To qualify for benefits a worker must have worked a minimum number of quarters in covered occupations. The minimum number depends on the age of the worker. Workers reaching age 62 in 1986 must have 35 quarters of coverage. The requirement will continue to increase by one quarter each year until 1991 when it reaches 40 quarters, or ten years. It will remain at 40 quarters thereafter.[1]

Monthly payments to retired workers are based on past earnings, not directly on past taxes. The benefit calculation procedure involves three steps.

Step 1: Taxable earnings for each year beginning with 1951 or the year the worker reaches age 21, whichever is later, and ending with the year before retirement are determined from Social Security Administration records. Earnings for each year prior to the two years before retirement are adjusted upward by a wage index. This procedure converts past earnings to close to their real value at time of retirement. Earnings during the last two calendar years before retirement are not indexed.

Step 2: Indexed earnings for the five lowest years are dropped. Earnings for the remaining years (the benefit calculation years) are summed and divided by the number of months in the benefit calculation years. For example, there are 30 benefit calculation years for a worker who retired in 1986. The sum of indexed earnings in these years is then divided by 360 (30 years × 12 months), yielding average indexed monthly earnings (AIME). The number of benefit calculation years will increase to a maximum of 35 in 1991 and remain at that level thereafter.

Step 3: The final step is to compute the primary insurance amount (PIA). The PIA is the monthly benefit that is paid to a worker without dependents who retires on reaching age 65. It is obtained by applying the benefit calculation formula to average indexed monthly earnings (AIME). The formula is progressive, resulting in higher benefits relative to earnings for workers with low average earnings. This is achieved by specifying three AIME brackets. Bracket limits, called bend points, are adjusted annually to reflect changes in average wages. Percentages do not vary. The formula used to calculate benefits for workers who retire in 1986 is:

90 percent of the first $297 of AIME, plus

32 percent of AIME in excess of $297 but less than $1,790, plus

15 percent of AIME in excess of $1,790.

Annual adjustments in bend points assure that the average size of new benefit awards grows at the same rate as average earnings of covered workers. Most retirees who worked full time in covered occupations fall into the second bracket. For workers retiring in 1986, the maximum PIA was $788.20. A special minimum benefit based only on years of coverage applies to a small number of workers with very low earnings and long periods of coverage.

The PIA serves as the basis for all benefit calculations. For example, workers opting for retirement at the minimum retirement age of 62 receive a benefit equal to 80 percent of PIA. This 20 percent reduction is an actuarial adjustment that is intended to compensate for the additional three years that workers who retire at 62 will draw benefits. The benefit reduction is prorated for workers who retire between ages 62 and 65. Workers who postpone retirement beyond age 65 receive a benefit increment of 3 percent per year (¼ of 1 percent for each month). The actuarial adjustment for early retirement is considered on average to be fair. The adjustment for late retirement is inadequate to compensate workers for lost benefits. It is anticipated that this inequity will eventually be eliminated when, starting in 1990, the delayed retirement credit will be raised gradually to 8 percent per year.

The PIA also provides a basis for calculation of dependent's and survivor's benefits. If a dependent spouse begins drawing benefits at age 65, the monthly payment is set at 50 percent of the working spouse's PIA. Spousal benefits are subject to the same actuarial adjustments for early and late retirement as worker's benefits. A dependent spouse cannot draw benefits until her (his) spouse is also retired. Additional dependents may be eligible for dependent's benefits if they are under age 18 and unmarried (or under age 19 and full-time high school students). Unmarried children over age 18 may qualify if they are in a severely disabled state that began before age 22. Dependent's benefits are constrained by a maximum total benefit payable to a family. The maximum ranges from 150 percent to 187 percent of PIA.

In many cases, both spouses are eligible for retirement benefits on their own accounts as well as for dependent's benefits. This is known as dual entitlement. In such cases, the individual receives only the larger of the two benefit payments.

Survivor's benefits are payable to surviving spouses and dependent children of deceased workers. Benefits are payable to widows or widowers aged 60 or over. Payments beginning at age 65 are equal to the worker's PIA. Monthly benefits are reduced if they begin before age 65. The reduction is equal to 30 percent of PIA if benefits begin at age 60.

A widow or widower under age 60 is eligible for survivor's benefits if he or she is caring for a child of the deceased worker under age 16. Surviving children are eligible for benefits if they are unmarried, under age 18 (age 19 if full-time high school students) or if they are in a severely disabled state that began before age 22.

Divorced spouses are generally eligible for survivor's or dependent's benefits if they were married to an eligible worker for 10 years or more. A divorced spouse who has been divorced for at least 2 years may begin drawing dependent's benefits at age 62 even if her (his) ex-spouse is not retired.

Since Social Security has historically been regarded as a form of earnings replacement, limits have been placed on benefits to persons who are still working but otherwise eligible for benefits. These restrictions, known as the "earnings test," have long been a source of controversy. Workers are allowed to earn an exempt amount without loss of benefits. The exempt amount is adjusted automatically in accordance with increases in average wages. For 1986 the amounts were $5,760 for beneficiaries under age 65 and $7,800 for beneficiaries aged 65 to 69. The test does not apply to workers aged 70 and over. The lower level for persons under age 65 is an additional penalty for early retirement. It also serves to limit benefits to surviving spouses with dependent children under age 16, since many such individuals find it necessary to work full time. Benefits are reduced by 50 cents for each dollar of earnings above the exempt level. The earnings test thus becomes a tax levied at a rate of 50 percent on affected earnings. When income and payroll taxes are added, the effective marginal tax rate on affected earnings creates a very strong work disincentive for eligible recipients. This is one reason why Congress in 1983 reduced the benefit reduction to $1 for $3 earnings beginning in 1990.[2]

Disability Insurance (DI). Disability insurance pays monthly cash benefits to insured persons who are totally disabled. In addition, persons who have received DI benefits for at least two consecutive years receive hospital and supplemental medical insurance under Medicare. There are three categories of disabled recipients. They include:

1. Insured workers under age 65 who become totally disabled with a disability that is expected to last for one year or more. Upon reaching age 65, such workers are transferred to OASI. Dependents of disabled workers may be eligible for dependent's benefits. Rules for determining the eligibility and level of dependent's benefits are identical to those under OASI. Dependent's benefits to spouses are subject to the earnings test.
2. Disabled widows or widowers aged 50 to 59 who meet other requirements for widow's or widower's benefits. Because these benefits begin at an earlier age than survivor's benefits, they are subject to an additional actuarial deduction.
3. Disabled children of an OASI or DI beneficiary. To qualify they must have become disabled before age 22. Benefits are payable after age 18.

Benefits are calculated in essentially the same way as OASI benefits. The only difference is in the procedure for determining the number of benefit calculation years. The DI program pays benefits to 2.7 million disabled workers and 1.3 million dependents. It accounts for about 9 percent of OASDHI expenditures. Each year more than one million workers apply for DI benefits. Less than half are found to be sufficiently disabled to qualify. Without strict standards the beneficiary roll would expand considerably. Many workers with physical or mental impairments have limited earning capacity, and this makes DI benefits an attractive alternative to working.

Attempts to reduce the drain on the DI fund by removing recipients from benefit status have met with limited success. Only modest numbers have been returned to the workforce through rehabilitation programs. The Reagan administration terminated payments to a number of recipients deemed capable of gainful activity. A political backlash led to passage of the Social Security Disability Benefits Reform Act of 1984. This act sets stricter guidelines for benefit termination. The Social Security Administration must demonstrate that a return to gainful activity is feasible because of improvement in the individual's medical condition, benefits from advances in medical technology or therapy, a finding through new diagnostic techniques that the individual is less disabled than previously thought, or that there was an error in the initial determination process. It is too early to evaluate the long-term effects of the new guidelines on program costs.

Medicare. The Medicare program includes two forms of insurance, hospital insurance (HI) and supplemental medical insurance (SMI). The HI component is financed by the payroll tax. It is available to eligible persons aged 65 and over, to disabled persons who have been entitled to disability insurance for 2 years or more, and to insured workers and their dependents who require dialysis or a transplant because of permanent kidney failure. HI pays a portion of the cost of inpatient hospital care and certain types of follow-up care. It accounts for about 11 percent of OASDHI outlays.

Persons who are eligible for HI may choose coverage under SMI. They must pay a monthly premium ($15.50 in 1986). Premiums cover less than 25 percent of costs. The remainder is paid out of the federal general fund. The share financed by premiums has declined continuously since payments began in 1966. In light of the Treasury subsidy, it is not surprising that nearly all eligible persons participate in SMI. It pays for a portion of the cost of physicians services, outpatient services of hospitals, and various other medical services and devices.

Among major items not covered by Medicare are dental expenses, eyeglasses and contact lenses, hearing aids, drugs and medicines not administered in hospitals, and custodial care in nursing homes.

Origin of the System

The United States was, according to one count, the thirtieth country to adopt a compulsory social insurance program.[3] The first was Germany in 1889. Spurred by European developments, social reformers in this country began campaigning for social insurance after the turn of the century. Campaigners expressed concern over the insecurity of workers in an industrialized economy. Low wages and intermittent unemployment made it impossible for workers to save for emergencies or retirement. A redistributive social insurance program was the answer.

During the 1920s attempts to arouse political support for unemployment and old age insurance were unsuccessful. Although the population of elderly was growing, it was not yet a political force. Private pension programs of trade unions and employers were coming into vogue, encouraged by favorable treatment under the federal income tax. Religious and fraternal organizations operated retirement homes. Among older males labor force participation rates were much higher than today's, limiting the need for earnings replacements. Local governments and a few states offered means-tested cash transfers to needy persons without other sources of support, and the county almshouses provided a shelter of last resort for indigent elderly.

The political atmosphere changed with the onset of the Great Depression. State governments provided the first line of defense, either by financing state programs or by enjoining local government to introduce or expand relief programs. The number of welfare recipients increased by more than twenty fold between 1930 and 1934, but benefit levels declined as state and local governments felt a revenue squeeze. This paved the way for federal intervention.

The Social Security Act of 1935. The centerpiece of the Social Security Act of 1935 was a compulsory program of retirement insurance to be administered by a federal agency, the Social Security Board. Coverage was extended to all employees in trade and industry, about two-thirds of the workforce. Among those not covered were the self-employed, farm workers, public sector employees, and railroad workers. The latter were covered by a previously established but similar federal program.

The system was to be financed by a flat-rate payroll tax applied to the first $3,000 of annual earnings. The tax applied equally to employer and employee at a rate of 1 percent on each. The maximum liability was thus $60. Tax collections began in 1937 with initial benefit payments to be delayed until 1942 to allow time for a trust fund to accumulate. Although workers with higher taxable earnings would receive more in benefits, those with lower earnings would receive a higher return per dollar of tax payments. This redistributive feature was assured by the benefit calculation formula and by a minimum benefit payable to all who qualify. Initial benefit payments would range from $10 to $25 per month but would increase gradually as the program matured.

In addition to OAI, the 1935 act provided for federal participation in unemployment insurance and public assistance. The unemployment insurance program was to be administered by the states, subject to federal guidelines, and to be financed by a payroll tax on employers in covered industries. Federal participation in public assistance was limited to two categories: old age assistance (OAA) and aid to dependent children (ADC). Administration remained in the hands of state and local welfare agencies. Federal subsidies would help to ease the financial burdens the Depression imposed on state and local treasuries.

OAA would offer income support for the many indigent elderly not eligible for Social Security, and it would supplement the income of Social Security beneficiaries with inadequate means. As the Social Security program matured it would gradually replace OAA for most beneficiaries. ADC would provide benefits for widows with dependent children. Recall that the original Social Security Act did not include survivor's benefits.

Goals of the Founders. Historians still debate the motives and goals of the system's founders. They all agree, however, that the emergence of compulsory social insurance in the United States was hastened and shaped by the experiences of the Great Depression. The Committee on Economic Security, or CES, was appointed in 1934 by President Franklin D. Roosevelt to draft the administration's proposal for a federal program of economic security. It was chaired by Frank Graham, president of the University of North Carolina. Other members were drawn from business and government. Only persons favorably inclined toward social insurance were appointed. One reason for drafting an administration bill was to forestall congressional action on legislation that would have provided federal subsidies to states that enacted old age pension laws. The administration favored a more comprehensive program that included social insurance.

The administration bill was drafted by the CES research staff, which was directed by Edward E. Witte, a professor of economics at the University of Wisconsin. The state of Wisconsin was a pioneer in social legislation and tax reform, and faculty from the university had a long tradition of involvement in public policy. Included in the administration's "economic security bill" were provisions for old age and unemployment insurance, matching grants to states with old age assistance programs, and a voluntary annuity program intended both as a supplement to social insurance and as a retirement alternative for workers not covered by the program. The annuity program was dropped by Congress, but the remaining provisions of the bill survived largely intact.

One significant change in the CES draft relates to funding. The tax-benefit package in the original draft was not self-financing. The CES proposal anticipated a modest fund accumulation to be supplemented with contributions from the general fund. Fiscal conservatives led by Secretary of the Treasury Henry Morgenthau pushed for a larger trust fund that would be fully financed by the payroll tax. Morgenthau, with presidential approval, prevailed. The combined employer-employee tax rate was set at 2 percent to be increased in stages to 6 percent by 1949. CES had proposed 1 percent with increases up to 5 percent by 1957. The program as passed by Congress was thought to approach actuarial soundness across generations, although this has been questioned. Because of the redistributive nature of the benefit formula, however, it would not approximate a private annuity program within generations.

The Social Security Act was signed by President Roosevelt on August 14, 1935. Administration of the program was placed under the control of the Social Security Board, a three-member panel. Its first chair, John Winant, was replaced within a year by Arthur J. Altmeyer. Altmeyer, like Witte, had been a University of Wisconsin faculty member. As a member of the CES staff he helped to draft the original legislation. Others from the CES research group remained to help staff the new agency. Altmeyer headed the board and its successor, the Social Security Administration, until 1953, and he exerted a major influence on the system during its formative years.

As indicated above, the Social Security system that emerged in 1935 is clearly a product of the Great Depression. It is recognized as a response to the needs of a generation that had seen much of its accumulated wealth dissipated by bank failures and the collapse of stock and real estate markets. The elderly could no longer count on financial support from their children, who were also experiencing economic distress. By encouraging older workers to retire, Social Security would open job opportunities to younger workers, and it would help to increase aggregate demand by maintaining the consumption of beneficiaries.

Two recent books offer different analyses of the emergence and evolution of Social Security. Both emphasize the key role played by the former academics and bureaucrats who were members of the CES research staff and who later dominated the SSB and its bureaucracy. Carolyn L. Weaver (1982) approaches the topic from a libertarian–public choice perspective; Jerry R. Cates (1983) provides a sociological and social work perspective.

Weaver links the originators of Social Security to social reformers of the early twentieth century. The most influential of these were Abraham Epstein and Isaac Rubinow. They emphasized the insecurity of workers inherent in a capitalistic wage system. Most workers are unable to save enough to protect themselves from earnings losses associated with unemployment, disability, and old age. Social justice requires a system of social insurance that assures a minimum standard of living for everyone. Through compulsory universal coverage, the risks of the labor market are shared by all members of the labor force. In order to assure a minimum living standard for all participants, the system must be tilted to favor workers with lower earnings. The necessary degree of redistribution can be achieved only through coercive state action.[4]

Weaver recites the historical record to support her contention that there was no broad base of support for the compulsory insurance program included in the 1935 act. Efforts to introduce social insurance during the 1920s failed even to get out of congressional committees. After the onset of the Great Depression strong support developed for federal subsidies to state and local relief programs. Support grew as unemployment skyrocketed and as the budgetary crises of state and local governments worsened.

At the same time grass-roots movements for more radical alternatives began to emerge. Huey Long's share-the-wealth movement was one example, but the most successful was that led by a California physician, Dr. Francis Townsend. He proposed a monthly pension of $200 for all persons over age 60. Recipients would be required to quit work and spend the money within a month. The pension, which was more than double the average monthly wage of the time, would be financed by a transactions tax.

In the face of these demands, the CES reported out a bill that linked compulsory social insurance with other more politically attractive features such as federal subsidies to state–local public assistance programs and state unemployment insurance. The administration, with the backing of the President, refused to consider disassembling the package, and a compliant Congress went along. The social insurance advocates got their program, then remained to administer the agency that was created to oversee its administration and eventual expansion.

Weaver sees the emergence of Social Security as the end product of a successful plan to control the congressional agenda and manipulate the flow of information. Only after the suppliers—the politicians and bureaucrats who wanted the program—had brought it into existence did public demand begin to develop. Over time, of course, substantial support emerged from the growing pool of beneficiaries.[5]

Whereas Weaver sees the founders of Social Security as successors to the early advocates of redistributionist social insurance, Cates sees them as fiscal conservatives striving to counter the threat from more radical alternatives. Of particular interest is his distinction between the "Wisconsin school," the system's founders, and earlier social insurance advocates like Epstein and Rubinow. The early advocates favored high minimum payments so as to insure decent living standards for all recipients. They realized that such a system would require substantial redistribution from high-earnings to low-earnings households. In effect the entire working population would share the risk of low earnings and earnings loss.[6]

Members of the Wisconsin school favored a program that would pay higher benefits to workers with higher prior earnings. Even with a progressive benefit formula and a low minimum benefit, Cates argues that this arrangement places a severe limit on the redistributive potential of the program. Both Cates and Weaver agree that the CES legislative package was designed to fend off proposals for large federal subsidies to state pension plans along with more radical redistributive programs like the Townsend plan.[7]

Cates supports his contention that the program's architects were conservative and anti-redistributionist by drawing upon the written records left behind by the participants. The many excerpts from these documents that are quoted in Cates' book offer convincing evidence of the devotion of the system's founders to a program of social insurance that tied benefits to prior earnings. It is worth mentioning, however, that the retirement insurance program contained in the 1935 Social Security Act is less redistributive, both across and within generations, than the program contained in the original CES draft. The reason for the difference is the adoption by Congress of the full-funding provision that was pushed by Morgenthau. In contrast, the CES version anticipated future general fund supplements, presumably financed by a progressive income tax.

Evolution of the System

Although the 1935 legislation introduced compulsory social insurance, the insurance terminology was suppressed until after the act passed the Supreme Court's test of constitutionality in 1937. Immediately thereafter the Social Security Board began to stress the analogy with private insurance. Tax payments were likened to premiums, to be returned as future benefits. Critics objected, pointing out that benefits were set by statute and were not contractual.

The 1939 Social Security Amendments: A Major Redirection. The 1939 Social Security Amendments represent a major departure from the original act. First, the amendments abandoned the principle of full reserve funding. Second, they weakened the link between tax payments and future benefits by introducing a more redistributive benefit formula and by adding survivor's and dependent's benefits.

The growing benefit reserve fund was seen as both an opportunity and a threat. To Congress and the administration it opened the possibility of beginning benefits sooner and raising benefit payments to early retirement cohorts. Some conservatives were worried about how a large fund might be invested. Not surprisingly, Congress responded by rescheduling initial benefit payments from 1942 to 1940. Survivors' benefits were added for dependent children and wives of deceased workers along with benefits for dependent spouses of retired workers. These changes tilted the benefit structure in favor of one-earner families over other participants, a feature that remains to this day.

Elimination of full reserve funding and use of the reserve account to increase benefits to early retirement cohorts moved the program toward a pay-as-you-go system. The system became a means of implementing inter-cohort redistribution. This in turn encouraged older voters and their lobbyists to press for repeated benefit increases. In time it would make the system more vulnerable to economic and demographic developments, although this was not generally understood in 1939.

Aside from a redirection in the goals of Social Security, the 1939 amendments introduced insurance terminology into the act. The 1935 legislation contained separate titles: Title II for benefits and Title VIII for the payroll tax. The two were separated for tactical reasons. It was hoped that the Supreme Court would find each title constitutional under congressional powers to tax and to appropriate. To link them in a public insurance program would be risky, particularly when facing a court that had found other New Deal programs to be unconstitutional. The tactic worked. The 1939 amendments replaced the old age reserve account in Title II with the old age and survivors insurance trust fund. Title VIII was amended to replace the payroll tax with insurance contributions under the Federal Insurance Contributions Act (FICA). FICA contributions were earmarked for the OASI Trust Fund. Weaver notes the irony in introducing insurance terminology in legislation that redirected Social Security away from the private insurance model.[8]

No major changes occurred during the 1940s. The tax rate remained at a combined rate of 2 percent on annual earnings up to $3,000. Although the typical retiree got back much more than he or she paid in taxes, benefits remained relatively low: they averaged about $25 per month by the end of the decade. High employment and a large ratio of workers to beneficiaries allowed for substantial fund accumulation. By 1950 the fund ratio (beginning balance as a percentage of annual benefit payments) reached 1,156, or 11.56 times the benefit liability for that year. Even at that time, however, the fund balance (after adding interest on U.S. government securities in which the fund was invested) would not have covered future benefit obligations already incurred.

The 1950s. The large fund balance was an irresistible temptation to Congress. The 1950 amendments granted current beneficiaries a 77.5 percent benefit increase. Eligibility requirements were relaxed. Compulsory coverage was extended to nonfarm, nonprofessional self-employed and to domestics. Benefit increases were easily accommodated, not only because of the large fund balance, but because of a favorable worker-beneficiary ratio. In 1950 there were six beneficiaries for every 100 workers; now there are more than 30. Congress nevertheless made one concession to conservative principles of finance. For the first time tax rates were increased. The combined employer-employee rate was raised to 3 percent; the newly covered self-employed paid a rate of 2.25 percent. The ceiling on taxable earnings remained at $3,000.

During the remainder of the decade the trend toward universal coverage continued. Among those added were farm operators and some farm employees, self-employed professionals other than physicians, and members of the armed forces. Voluntary coverage was extended to employees covered by state and local government retirement systems and to employees of religious and other nonprofit organizations. Disability insurance for totally disabled workers was added in 1956. Initially, disability benefits were payable only after age 50. Minimum age for OASI benefits to women was reduced from 65 to 62. Benefits were increased three times between 1952 and 1958, and by the end of the decade the combined employer-employee tax rate stood at 4.5 percent on earnings up to $4,800. The rate on the self-employed was 3.75 percent.

The 1960s. As the system matured, the number of beneficiaries per 100 workers continued to rise, reaching twenty by 1960, twenty-five by 1965, and thirty by 1969. Benefit payments tripled; the combined tax rate on employers and employees advanced to 5.4 percent; and the ceiling on taxable earnings was raised in stages to $7,800.

During the decade Presidents John F. Kennedy and Lyndon Johnson initiated a series of proposals for expanding income maintenance and support programs for the elderly and disadvantaged. The most important was Medicare, a program of hospital insurance and supplementary medical insurance. After a lengthy political struggle Medicare was approved by Congress in 1965, and payments to eligible persons aged 65 and over began in July 1966. Minimum age of eligibility for Disability Insurance was lowered to age 31 in 1960 and to age 22 in 1967. In 1962 the minimum retirement age for men was lowered to 62. Over the decade a series of ad hoc benefit increases, coupled with higher average earnings of newly retired workers, raised average benefits by 59 percent.

In this atmosphere it is not surprising that influential persons in Congress and the administration should be pushing for an expanded role for Social Security. Among the leaders of this group was Robert M. Ball, commissioner of Social Security from 1962 to 1973. Ball favored a Social Security program that would provide not just an income floor, but a major share of the retirement income of nearly all working people. By the late 1960s the expansionary drive was well underway, and efforts of fiscal conservatives in the Nixon administration and in Congress to contain it would prove to be ineffective.[9] The drive to expand began with approval in 1969 of a 15 percent benefit increase, effective January 1, 1970. This increase was accommodated without any revision of previously scheduled payroll tax rate increases.

Restructuring the System: 1971–77. The benefit increase implemented in 1970 was followed by a 10 percent increase, effective in January 1971. This increase required the raising of both the tax rate and taxable earnings ceiling. These benefit increases far exceeded advances in cost of living, but they did not entail a departure from the financing procedures followed in the 1950s and 1960s.

Prior to 1972 Social Security Administration actuaries based estimates of future funding needs on the "level earnings" assumption, the conservative assumption that taxable earnings would remain at current levels instead of rising. Since earnings did in fact rise, this scheme always generated an actuarial surplus that could be used to pay for future benefit increases. This method of finance was strongly supported by Chief Actuary Robert J. Myers and by the House Ways and Means Committee and its chairman, Wilbur Mills of Arkansas. The Ways and Means Committee and its Senate counterpart, the Finance Committee, are responsible for originating Social Security legislation. The break with the past occurred in 1972. An amendment increasing benefits by 20 percent was attached to a bill raising the debt limit. The benefit increase was rushed through Congress outside normal committee channels, but with the approval of Mills and Finance Committee Chairman Russell Long of Louisiana. The benefit increase was linked to a modest increase in the taxable earnings ceiling and would not have been allowed under the level earnings criterion.

Under the new earnings assumption, Congress gambled that future growth in taxable earnings would generate enough revenue to cover benefit increases. This was the first step toward tying the financial health of the system to the performance of the economy.

Two developments facilitated the move away from the conservative "level earnings" method of actuarial accounting. One was the resignation in 1970 of SSA Chief Actuary Myers. His departure marked the end of major internal opposition to Commissioner Ball's plans for program expansion, and it removed the most effective proponent of conservative financing. The other was the strong recommendation of the 1971 Social Security Advisory Council that the "static" earnings assumption of the level earnings approach be replaced by a "dynamic" assumption that earnings would rise at a forecasted rate.

The Advisory Council report played down the argument that benefit increases could threaten the solvency of the trust funds if the forecasts were too optimistic. Indeed, the change in the earnings assumption encountered little opposition. Representative John Byrnes of Wisconsin, ranking Republican on the Ways and Means Committee, delivered an impassioned warning during the House debate, but the opposition was overwhelmed in both the House and Senate.

One reason for the lack of attention to the change in the actuarial accounting method was the diversion of attention to another issue, indexing, which ties benefit increases to increases in the cost of living. Indexing of benefits drew support from across the political spectrum. Expansionists like Ball saw it as a way of complementing their plans for a bigger and better system. Fiscal conservatives looked upon indexing as a means of controlling benefit increases by avoiding the regular and politically inspired benefit increases that were ushered through Congress.

In October 1972, three months after approval of the 20 percent benefit increase, Congress passed the Social Security Amendments of 1972. This legislation raised the 1973 tax rate and provided benefit increases for widows and widowers. It also liberalized the earnings test and shortened the waiting period for disability insurance. Its major feature, however, was the indexing of both benefits and the ceiling on taxable earnings. Benefit increases were tied to increases in the cost of living, as measured by the consumer price index. Increases in the taxable earnings ceiling were tied to a wage index for workers in covered occupations.

Automatic indexing was to begin in 1973, but early in that year Congress postponed it until 1975. In its place Congress substituted two additional legislated benefit increases and raised the ceiling on taxable earnings. By 1975 the combined OASDHI tax rate on employers and employees was 11.7 percent on a maximum base of $14,100. The maximum tax liability of $1,649.70 may be compared to $60 at the program's inception.

Unfortunately, the newly indexed benefit structure and the accompanying payroll tax failed to work as anticipated. The indexing formula written into the 1972 amendments contained a technical flaw that overadjusted for inflation. An unanticipated increase in disability awards threatened the DI fund. Worst of all, stagflation—a combination of high unemployment, slow growth, and inflation—caused payroll tax revenues to fall short of benefit payments. The 1972 amendments had established benefit and tax schedules with automatic adjustments but without a direct linkage, making the system much more susceptible to a funding crisis. The crisis came in 1977, and Congress was forced to act.

The 1977 Social Security Amendments. The Social Security Amendments of 1977 retained the major features of the earlier legislation. These include enhanced benefit levels (increments well in excess of increases in cost of living) and automatic adjustment of benefits and the tax base in accordance with predetermined formulas. The flaw in the indexing procedure that overadjusted for inflation was eliminated. Larger future tax increases were built into the system. It was thought that these changes would assure the solvency of the system well into the next century.

An adequate margin of safety would get us through the 1980s, even if the most pessimistic economic and demographic projections of SSA actuaries were realized. After 1990 sizable trust fund surpluses would accumulate. These would provide a cushion for the pressures on the system that would develop when the baby-boom generation began reaching retirement age after 2010. Some sort of adjustment might be needed to deal with that situation, but that could be postponed until we had a better feel for the economic and demographic trends of the next century.

One feature of the 1977 amendments is of particular interest. This is the decision to use two forms of indexing. One form, called wage indexing, is used to calculate the initial monthly benefit awarded to a worker at retirement (or on becoming eligible for disability benefits). The other form, called price indexing, is used to make annual cost-of-living adjustments for persons already receiving benefits.

The formula for calculating initial monthly benefits has been described above. Under wage indexing each successive cohort receives an initial benefit award that is a constant percentage of its prior taxable earnings. The percentage for each worker, however, depends on his or her earnings relative to others in the same cohort. In keeping with the redistributive nature of the Social Security benefit structure, the percentage declines as average earnings rise.

For example, a worker retiring at the regular retirement age (currently 65 but scheduled to rise to 67 by 2022) with lifetime earnings equal to the average for his or her cohort will receive retirement benefits equal to approximately 44 percent of earnings during the last full year of work before retirement. If the worker also receives dependent's benefits for a nonworking spouse of normal retirement age, benefits will equal 66 percent of the last year's earnings. This percentage does not change over generations. Consequently, if real earnings were to double over the next 50 years, Social Security benefits for a newly retired worker would also double in real terms. This is the intent of wage indexing.

The 44 percent figure is called the replacement rate, since it gives the percentage of gross (before-tax) earnings that are replaced by Social Security. The replacement rate for a low-wage worker is approximately 55 percent. With full spouse's benefits it would be about 83 percent. For a worker with earnings equal to the taxable maximum each year, the corresponding replacement rates are about 30 percent for a worker and 45 percent for a worker receiving full spouse's benefits. Social Security is now designed to provide the major source of retirement income for most retirees, particularly for those in the lower and middle income ranges. This is the goal envisioned by Commissioner Ball and his supporters when they began the drive for the program expansion in the 1960s.

By 1981 it was obvious that the 1977 amendments were inadequate. Benefit payments were outpacing payroll tax receipts as wage increases lagged behind inflation. Rising unemployment added to the system's troubles. In an effort to forestall the inevitable, several benefit cutbacks were included in the Omnibus Budget Reconciliation Act of 1981. These included a phase-out of survivor's benefits for post-secondary students over age 18, cessation of benefits to surviving parents when dependent children reach age 16 rather than 18, a cap on DI benefits, and other minor changes.

Four months later, in December 1981, additional amendments to the Social Security Act were approved. The minimum benefit for retired persons with very low earnings, which had been eliminated by the Reconciliation Act, was restored for workers who retired before 1982. Interfund borrowing was authorized in order to rescue the OASI Trust Fund from a looming shortfall. Payroll tax liability was extended to the first six months of sick pay. These changes averted disaster until after the 1982 election.

The 1983 Amendments. The recommendations of the National Commission on Social Security Reform were released on January 20, 1983. Its recommendations served as the basis for the Social Security Amendments of 1983. The Commission was established by executive order of President Ronald Reagan on December 16, 1981 "to propose realistic, long-term reforms to put Social Security back on a sound financial footing" and to "forge a working, bipartisan consensus so that the necessary reforms can be passed into law." The latter feature was important, because it was obvious that taxes would have to be raised and future benefits would have to be cut in order to restore the financial soundness of the system.

The Commission was composed of 15 members; five each were appointed by President Reagan, Senate Majority Leader Howard Baker, and Speaker of the House of Representatives Thomas P. O'Neill. It was chaired by economist Alan Greenspan. Its bipartisan membership included current and former members of Congress, representatives of business and labor, and former Social Security Commissioner Robert M. Ball. The Commission's report was conveniently delayed until after the 1982 Congressional elections. President Reagan, in his state-of-the-union address on January 25, 1983, urged Congress to enact the Commission plan by Easter. The Commission's recommendations emerged essentially intact in the 1983 Social Security Amendments, which were signed by President Reagan on April 20, 1983.[10]

The major provisions pertaining to benefits may be summarized briefly:

1. Compulsory coverage was extended to new federal employees hired after January 1, 1984, to members of Congress, the President and Vice President, federal judges, most political appointees in the executive branch, and employees of the legislative branch. Compulsory coverage was also extended to most employees of nonprofit organizations. State and local governments are no longer allowed to remove employees from coverage, and employees whose previous coverage had been terminated may now elect to be covered again. This provision is a major step toward full coverage of the labor force.

2. The cost-of-living adjustment (COLA) due in July 1983 was delayed until January 1984. This six-month delay results in a permanent reduction for current beneficiaries. If the trust fund drops below a triggering level of 20 percent of annual benefits (15 percent through 1988), the COLA adjustment will be based on the smaller of (1) the increase in the consumer price index or (2) an index of covered wages. The full adjustment would be restored if, at a future date, the trust fund ratio reaches 32 percent. The purpose of this provision is to protect the trust fund during periods when prices are rising faster than wages. This occurred during the period 1972–82 and contributed to the funding crisis.

3. A special benefit calculation formula was added for workers with short work histories under Social Security. This provision is directed mainly at Civil Service "double-dippers" who benefit from the redistributive nature of the benefit formula.

4. The withholding rate for benefits subject to the earnings test is to be reduced from $1 for each $2 of earnings over the annual exempt amount to $1 for each $3 of excess earnings, beginning in 1990. This relaxation applies only to workers who attain full retirement age (currently 65) and is intended to moderate the work-disincentive effect of the earnings test.

5. The delayed retirement credit, currently 3 percent per year for each year of delayed retirement beyond age 65, will gradually be increased to 8 percent between 1987 and 2004.

For the first time a portion of Social Security benefit payments is now subject to the income tax. The base amounts for determining taxable benefits are $25,000 for a single taxpayer, $32,000 for married couples filing jointly, and zero for married taxpayers filing separately. Income for purposes of figuring the base amounts includes adjusted gross income plus nontaxable interest income plus one-half of Social Security benefits. The amount of benefits included in taxable income is the lesser of one-half of Social Security benefits or one-half of income over the base amount. Revenue collected under this provision is returned to the Social Security Trust Fund. Its effect is to place a part of the burden of supporting each retirement generation on the more affluent members of their own generation, thereby reducing intergeneration transfers and lowering the burden on younger working generations.

The budget provisions of the 1983 amendments included some liberalizations in benefit eligibility requirements. Benefits are no longer terminated for divorced spouses and disabled widows or widowers who remarry. A divorced spouse who has been divorced for at least two years may now apply for dependent's benefits regardless of whether the former spouse has retired or has benefits withheld under the earnings test.

On the revenue side, the amendments accelerated the application of tax increases scheduled under previous law. Tax rates on self-employed persons were raised to the same level as the combined employer-employee rate. These rates previously had been scheduled to equal 75 percent of OASDI and 50 percent of HI rates on employees. This change is partially offset by income tax credits (for the years 1984–89) against the income tax liability of the self employed. After 1989, self-employed persons will be allowed an income tax deduction equal to one-half the self-employment payroll tax. This feature parallels tax treatment of the employer's share of the employer-employee tax. Since the provision reduces the income tax liability of the self-employed, it provides an indirect general fund subsidy to the OASDHI trust funds.

A major feature designed to deal with the projected long-term trust fund deficit is the provision delaying the normal retirement age. The age at which full retirement benefits are available will be advanced from the current 65 by two months a year to age 66 during the years 2000–2005. Workers reaching age 62 before 2000 are not affected. The normal retirement age remains at 66 until 2017, when it is again increased by 2 months per year until 2022, at which point it will be fixed at age 67. The second phased increase in retirement age affects workers reaching age 62 in 2017 and thereafter. The actuarial reduction for retirement at age 62, now 20 percent, will be increased in stages along with the retirement age. The reduction will reach 30 percent when the retirement age is set at age 67. Advancement of normal retirement age will result in a benefit cut for all beneficiaries born in 1938 or later. The benefit cut is greatest for persons born in 1960 or later.

Long-Term Prospects

The revenue-enhancing provisions of the 1983 Social Security Amendments appear to have put the OASDI trust funds on a sound footing for at least the next 25 years. Actuarial projections indicate, however, that a repeat of the high inflation, high unemployment, and declining real wages experienced between 1979 and 1982 could again send the funds into insolvency before the end of the decade. While this is considered unlikely, long-term funding problems for OASDI are a possibility and, indeed, are considered likely. The hospital insurance fund is headed for insolvency by the 1990s under all but the most optimistic projections. No long-term projections are made for supplementary medical insurance, which is financed by general fund appropriations and premiums from beneficiaries.[11]

The prospects for the trust funds hinge on a variety of interacting economic variables, demographic trends, and program parameters. Payroll tax revenues depend on the size of the working-age population, labor force participation and employment rates, and earnings. Earnings and employment are in turn dependent on the skills of the labor force, capital formation, and technological change. These are the underlying determinants of labor productivity.

Payroll taxes are supplemented by interest on trust fund assets and earmarked revenue from the income tax on Social Security benefits. Interest income is of little consequence at current fund levels but could become substantial if fund accumulation is allowed over the next two decades. A policy of fund accumulation offers one option for meeting the benefit drain that will occur after 2010. Receipts from the income tax on benefits are difficult to predict, since it is unlikely that Congress will retain the existing base amounts ($25,000 for single persons, $32,000 for married couples filing jointly) in the face of even modest rates of inflation.

Seventy-Five-Year Projections

Benefit payments from the OASI fund are influenced by earnings histories, the benefit calculation formula, retirement decisions and job opportunities for older workers, and mortality rates. Payments from the DI fund depend on the disability rate, the rigor of the disability determination process, the degree of success in occupational rehabilitation, and mortality rates among disabled workers.

Each year Social Security Administration actuaries publish a set of trust fund projections for the next 75 years. Estimates are based on four sets of assumptions. Alternative I is the most optimistic. Economic assumptions include real growth rates in excess of 3 percent per year, substantial growth in real earnings (exceeding 2 percent per year), and unemployment rates that fall from present levels to about 5 percent by 1990. A steady decline in the rate of inflation to a stable rate of 2 percent after 1992 is projected. While such a performance is not inconceivable, it is better than our record since the 1960s. Demographic assumptions are also more favorable to the system than recent experience. These include higher fertility rates and smaller increases in life expectancies than the other alternatives. This means a higher ratio of workers to beneficiaries in the future.

Alternative III is the most pessimistic. Economic assumptions include sluggish growth (real growth in GNP of generally less than 2 percent per year and dropping to 0.7 percent in 75 years), annual inflation rates at about 5 percent, and unemployment rates at about 7 percent. Demographic assumptions include a small decline in the fertility rate combined with longer life expectancies. Should these projections materialize, the OASDI program would have 57 beneficiaries per 100 covered workers by 2025, in contrast to the current 30. By 2060 there would be 83 beneficiaries for each 100 workers.

The alternative I and III projections are intended to provide a set of reasonable upper and lower limits to actual performance. Two sets of intermediate projections are intended to approximate the more likely paths of economic and demographic variables. Alternatives IIA and IIB share the same intermediate demographic projections, including a small rise in fertility and modest increases in life expectancy. Economic projections are more optimistic under IIA. Real growth of between 2.3 and 3.1 percent per year is projected for the period 1991–2060. This is combined with long-term inflation rates of 3 percent per year and unemployment rates of 5.5 percent. The less optimistic IIB projections include growth rates that generally decline from 2.9 percent per year in 1991 to 1.9 percent in 2060. Higher inflation (4 percent per year) and unemployment (6 percent) are projected for most of the 75-year projection period.

The implications of the four alternatives for the long-term solvency of the OASDI trust funds can be seen by examining figure 1–1. Projected fund outlays as a percentage of taxable payroll are shown for each alternative, along with the payroll tax rate under legislation in effect in 1986. Alternative III shows a small surplus until the second decade of the next century. Thereafter the deficit mounts continuously, exceeding 12 percent of payroll by 2060. These projections indicate a need for major restructuring by 2010.

The intermediate projections show a fund surplus until well into the second decade of the next century. At that time demographics turn against

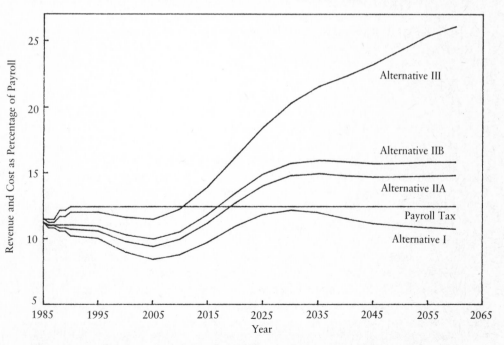

Figure 1–1. Revenue and Cost of OASDI as a Percentage of Taxable Payroll

the system and deficits of about 1.6 percent (IIA) to 2.6 percent (IIB) of payroll prevail after about 2030.

In contrast, the optimistic projection, alternative I, shows the funds in surplus for each of the 75 years between 1985 and 2060. Only around the year 2030 does the margin between revenue and expenditures narrow to less than 1 percent of payroll.

The projections include estimated revenues from the income tax on benefits, which is rechanneled back into the trust funds. In nearly all cases projected revenue from this source amounts to less than 1 percent of payroll and therefore does not appreciably affect the pattern of surpluses and deficits. In order to simplify the graphics, only legislated payroll tax receipts are shown in figure 1–1.

The projections indicate that in the absence of strong economic performance and favorable demographics the Social Security system will fail to provide legislated OASI and DI benefits to the "baby-boom" generation unless tax revenues are increased. Accommodation at reasonable cost to taxpayers and beneficiaries may be feasible if developments within the range of intermediate projections are realized, but legislated benefits could be maintained only at great cost to the working generations if the economic and demographic trends are less favorable.

The prospects for the OASI and DI trust funds are only part of the story. Prospects for the future of Medicare are less favorable. Projections are made only for the hospital insurance (HI) component, the portion financed by the payroll tax. The ratio of HI expenditures to payroll rose for 0.94 percent of taxable payroll in 1967 to 2.61 percent in 1985. Since the legislated HI tax rate is set at 2.9 percent of payroll for 1986 and subsequent years, growth rates approaching those of the past two decades will cause outlays to outstrip revenues even under the most optimistic projections.

Actuarial projections under intermediate (alternative IIA and IIB) and pessimistic (alternative III) assumptions show a deficit in the HI fund early in the 1990s. By the end of the decade projected deficits are well in excess of $20 billion per year. Optimistic assumptions (alternative I) show a fund in precarious balance until 2010. Long-term projections for the HI fund are difficult to make for several reasons. They are sensitive to assumptions about longevity and incidence of disability, as well as to developments in medical technology. The effect of recent changes in hospital reimbursement procedures and of efforts to control hospital expenses are not well understood at this time. Nevertheless, there is widespread agreement that HI payroll tax rates will have to be increased soon to keep the fund in balance.

Some observers are predicting a funding crisis in Medicare, including the optional supplemental medical insurance (SMI) fund, which is financed from general revenues and beneficiary premiums. A former chief actuary of the Social Security Administration, A. Haeworth Robertson, projects SMI expenditures that will eventually equal 5 percent of taxable earnings.[12]

Table 1–3
Projected Cost of Old Age, Survivors, Disability, and Health Insurance as a
Percentage of Taxable Payroll for Selected Time Intervals

| | *Actuarial Assumptions*[a] | | | |
	I	IIA	IIB	III
1986–2010				
OASDI	9.41	10.12	10.54	11.70
HI	2.96	3.56	3.72	4.87
OASDHI	12.37	13.68	14.26	16.57
2011–2035				
OASDI	11.06	13.10	13.91	17.33
HI	3.34	5.76	6.18	11.85
OASDHI	14.40	18.86	20.09	29.18
2036–2060				
OASDI	11.08	14.71	15.74	23.91
HI	3.96	7.33	7.86	16.06
OASDHI	15.04	22.04	23.60	39.97
1986–2060				
OASDI	10.52	12.64	13.40	17.64
HI	3.42	5.55	5.92	10.93
OASDHI	13.94	18.19	19.32	28.57

Source: U.S. Congress, Committee on Ways and Means (1986a), p. 49; U.S. Congress, Committee on Ways and Means (1986b), pp. 65–66.

[a] Alternative I: optimistic; alternatives IIA and IIB: intermediate; alternative III: pessimistic.

Some implications of the actuarial projections are revealed in table 1–3. Costs are shown as a percentage of taxable payroll, averaged over the three 25-year intervals comprising the period 1986–2060. Estimates are shown separately for OASDI and HI and for the combined funds. As a reminder, legislated payroll taxes are scheduled to stabilize at 15.3 percent of payroll beginning in 1990. For the first 25-year period, 1986–2010, the projections are optimistic. Only under a "worst-case" scenario will taxes have to be raised. During the second 25-year period (2011–2035), tax increases are likely unless economic and demographic factors are highly favorable. A sluggish economy and unfavorable demographics would require sizable tax increases or benefit cuts to maintain solvency. Pressure on the fund increases after 2035 under all alternatives, but only the pessimistic outcome (alternative III) would require the tax rates of 40 percent of payroll (not counting SMI) expected by some alarmists.

Perhaps it is worth noting that the HI fund is the major contributor to the projected deficit after 2010 (and earlier under alternative III assumptions). For the period 2036–2060 the HI deficit ranges from 0.52 percent of taxable payroll under alternative IIA assumptions to 13.16 percent of payroll under alternative III assumptions. Thus roughly 60 percent of the disastrous alternative III deficit for that period is attributable to hospital costs.

Remember that these figures are projections, not predictions. Long-term demographic trends are notoriously difficult to predict, and no one knows how the U.S. economy will perform over the next three-quarters of a century. One reason why critics of the program take the long-term pessimistic projections seriously is that they perceive a connection between Social Security and a sluggish economy. Social Security is alleged to stifle economic growth by discouraging saving and the supply of work effort. We consider this and other reasons for a phase-out of Social Security in the next section.

Is Social Security Outdated?

Colin Campbell once described Social Security as a program in search of an explanation.[13] To seek an explanation, one must turn to the historical record. To seek a justification, one may turn to the economic theory of market failure.

It is sometimes argued that Social Security came into existence in the 1930s because workers of that generation realized that it would yield them a great windfall. Because of pay-as-you-go financing, early retirees would enjoy benefits financed by payroll taxes paid by younger workers. The low cost of the program during its early years, coupled with sympathy for a generation buffeted by the Great Depression, served to dampen opposition among younger workers.

Our historical survey casts doubt upon this explanation. The 1935 act was thought to be largely self-financed within generations. The transition to pay-as-you-go did not begin until 1939 and was not fully implemented until 1950. Furthermore, given the emphasis on the insurance analogy, it is unlikely that most early or even current beneficiaries fully recognized the magnitude of the windfall they were to receive.[14] The historical record indicates that by 1935 strong support existed for some form of federally sanctioned earnings replacement for the elderly and unemployed. The program that emerged, a combination of social insurance and federally subsidized public assistance, helped meet the needs of a Depression decade. It also served to block efforts to introduce a more redistributive alternative.

The glory days of Social Security, roughly the period 1950–1972, were marked by benefit windfalls and relatively modest tax rates. Those days are gone, and since 1977 Congress has twice been forced to act to fend off financial disaster. Actuarial projections indicate that future crises are possible and, some would say, likely.[15]

Is Social Security outdated and destined to disappear? Can it be justified? Political support remains strong, abetted by a large and growing bloc of older voters. Many economists continue to defend compulsory social insurance as a necessary corrective for market failure in markets for retirement annuities and insurance against earnings loss. Support also comes from those who favor its social adequacy provisions, particularly when contrasted to means-tested alternatives. These and other arguments are evaluated in chapter 6. We turn now to the case for a phase out.

Radical Reform

A number of plans have been devised for radical reform of our system of social insurance. The less extreme call for transition to a fully funded and compulsory public system, a compulsory private system, or a voluntary public system.[16] A fully funded public system would channel contributions of each working cohort into a fund that would be invested in government securities (and perhaps other financial instruments). Benefits to the cohort would then be paid out of the accumulated fund. Intercohort redistribution would be eliminated, but redistribution within cohorts would be possible. Under this reform, Social Security would return to the form prescribed in the original 1935 Social Security Act. The transition to full funding would have to be extended over several decades, because it would require workers to finance both their own retirement and that of current beneficiaries of the existing pay-as-you-go system. The reason for full funding is to eliminate the depressing effect on saving and capital formation that is alleged to occur under pay-as-you-go financing.[17]

A compulsory private system would of necessity be fully funded, since private insurers could not finance benefits to noncontributors. It would differ from a fully funded public system in two ways. First, workers' benefits would be based strictly on their previous contributions and would reflect standards of actuarial fairness. There would be no redistribution. Second, private firms would be able to invest funds in a wider variety of investment outlets without fear of political control over allocation of capital. Again, the transition to full funding would take decades.

A voluntary public program would grant individuals the right to purchase rights to benefits that would be guaranteed by the federal government. A meaningful voluntary program should offer options that are not available from the private sector. A likely option would be bonds that yield a low real return but that are indexed against inflation. Even with a low real yield, indexed bonds would offer investors an inflation hedge that cannot be matched by the private sector. On reaching retirement, the individual could convert the bonds to indexed annuities or dispose of the proceeds in other ways. Note that a voluntary program allows each individual to decide how much, if anything, to save for retirement. It also precludes redistribution, because likely losers would choose not to participate.

All of the arrangements described above involve major departures from the current Social Security system, but proposals to phase-out Social Security represent the most radical departure from present policy. Eventually all functions of the Social Security system would shift to the private sector, and all provision for earnings loss and medical care would come under private, voluntary control. The government could retain a residual role by, for example, regulating private insurers or granting tax breaks on contributions to retirement accounts and pension funds.

The chapters that follow examine the economic implications and political feasibility of a phase-out. The most thorough and well-conceived of the phase-out proposals is that of Peter J. Ferrara.[18] It serves as the basis for the critique that will follow. The remainder of this section is devoted to a summary of arguments in favor of eliminating our nearly universal system of compulsory social insurance, followed by a description of the Ferrara plan.

The Case for a Phase-Out

Those who favor a phase-out of Social Security base their argument on one or more of the following features or perceived consequences of the program: its compulsory nature, its harmful effect on the economy, or the way it redistributes income across or within generations.

Compulsion. Under Social Security workers are required to participate in a program whose basic features are collectively determined. They are deprived of the freedom to plan for their own economic security in a manner consistent with their own preferences and circumstances. A form of "forced" saving limits control over the timing and means of accumulation. Penalties for late or early retirement and the earnings test interfere with the free exercise of labor supply decisions.

Critics find the compulsory nature of the system paternalistic and degrading. They concede that some people may not save enough to finance their retirement, but one of the rights in a free society is the right to make one's own mistakes. Ferrara adds that if it becomes apparent that savings are inadequate, one can always continue working.[19] Labor force participation rates of older males were much higher before Social Security and may rise again if the system is phased out. A welfare safety net could offer protection for destitute elderly who can no longer work. Alternatively, workers could protect themselves through the purchase of private disability insurance.[20]

The emphasis on freedom from coercion derives from the classical theory of individual rights as articulated by philosophers from John Locke to Robert Nozick. Collectivist efforts to provide security for everyone entail a violation of the fundamental rights of property, association, and contract.[21]

Pay-As-You-Go Finance. Much of the opposition to Social Security centers on the implications of pay-as-you-go finance. As we have seen, the 1939

Social Security amendments abandoned full funding, and the 1950 amendments completed the transition to a pay-as-you-go system.

Proponents of full funding see the present system as a form of "compulsory nonsaving." A funded system, either public or private, would create a large fund that could be invested in productive capital. It would presumably increase capital formation even if invested only in government securities. The fund could absorb an increasing share of our huge public debt, thereby freeing private savings for private capital formation. If current benefit obligations were fully funded, however, the size of the fund would exceed the current federal debt, perhaps by three or four times. Thus most of the fund would be invested in the private sector. Fear of such a development caused conservatives to oppose full funding in the 1940s, and it is another reason why some radical reformers want to phase in a fully private retirement system.

In contrast to a funded system, our present arrangement is alleged to reduce the need for saving and dissipate a larger share of our national product into current consumption. This is because Social Security reduces the need of workers to save for retirement. A move toward a funded system would stem this dissipation and contribute to what Ferrara calls a "supply-side boom."[22]

Intercohort and Intracohort Redistribution. As described in our historical sketch, the transition to pay-as-you-go finance made possible the massive intergenerational transfers to past and current retirement cohorts. As the system matures these windfalls will disappear. Real returns to cohorts retiring after the first decade of the next century could drop to 1 or 2 percent, perhaps even less. Because the system redistributes within cohorts, large numbers of participants can anticipate negative returns. Among the likely losers are the more affluent, especially in two-earner households, and groups with less favorable survival probabilities, most notably single males.

In contrast to the high returns on savings invested in the private sector, Social Security will look like a poor bargain. Ferrara, for example, points to an average 12 percent before-tax return to private investment. Even if taxes on business income and property reduce the real net return to 7 or 8 percent, private investments will look much more attractive, especially if they can be invested in tax-deferred retirement accounts.[23]

Phase-Out. Once younger workers become aware of these numbers, Ferrara and others foresee a massive erosion of political support for the present system. A phase-out will become an attractive option even with the necessity to retain the pay-as-you-go system for current beneficiaries and for older workers who do not have time to accumulate adequate retirement accounts.

In time all functions now performed by the Social Security system would shift to the private sector. All provision for earnings loss from retirement or disability and for medical care for the elderly would come under private, voluntary control. We turn next to an exposition of the Ferrara plan, which will serve as the basis for our critique.

The Ferrara Plan

Ferrara proposes to phase out the existing pay-as-you-go Social Security system and to replace it with a fully funded private system. A private system, he contends, would yield higher returns, especially to baby boomers and their successors. It would be immune to the periodic funding crises that plague the existing system. Ferrara recognizes that the chief obstacle to a transition is the political necessity of paying off current benefit obligations while saving for a reserve fund. Younger workers must be convinced that they can pay taxes to meet existing obligations, accumulate savings for their own retirement, and come out ahead in the long run. This is possible because of the large economic gains that reform will create for younger workers. Current obligations can be met by capturing only a portion of these gains. Hence the phase-out will be self financing.

Ferrara has offered three plans for implementing a phase-out. The first and most radical was published in 1980. In deference to political concerns he offered in 1982 what he termed a "measured alternative." His "Super IRA" plan, published in 1985, is similar in form but even more modest in inception. All three plans would lead to eventual phase out of the current system. The summary that follows considers only the 1980 and 1985 versions.

The 1980 Version

This plan includes both short-run and long-run reforms.[24] The short-run reforms are intended to cut program costs immediately in order to make long-run reforms easier and less costly.

The following short-run reforms would eliminate welfare (redistributive) elements from Social Security.

1. Each old age insurance (OAI) beneficiary would get back only the amount paid in as taxes plus accumulated interest. The portion of payroll taxes assigned to pay for survivor's insurance (SI), disability insurance (DI), and hospital insurance (HI) would be treated like private insurance premiums. Future SI, DI, and HI benefits would depend solely on past premiums, i.e., past taxes. Supplemental security income (SSI) benefits would be increased to shield beneficiaries from economic deprivation. Since SSI is a means-tested welfare program, public transfers to the nonneedy would be eliminated.

2. Eliminate spousal and dependent's benefits under OAI and DI. This

feature is implicit in the benefit rules cited above. According to Ferrara, this change would eliminate the chief source of inequity between individuals and families.

3. Eliminate maximum family benefits and minimum benefits. Again, this follows from the redefined benefit rules.

4. Eliminate the earnings test for workers eligible for benefits. The earnings test is consistent with the principle that Social Security is a form of earnings replacement, but it is not consistent with the private insurance principle.

These changes would be phased in gradually and would not apply to retired workers or to older members of the work force, since these individuals would not be able to accumulate sufficient privately funded retirement accounts. For those affected by the changes, the interest accumulations, in so far as the interest rates include an inflation adjustment, would insure the real purchasing power of previous tax payments.

Ferrara suggests two other short-run reforms that could lower future benefit obligations. One would replace wage indexing with price indexing in the benefit formula. Because of rising labor productivity, wages tend to increase more rapidly over time than prices. If average indexed monthly earnings are obtained through price indexing, benefit payments would be reduced. The long-term effect is to reduce benefit payments *relative* to average wages. In contrast, wage indexing holds benefits constant *relative* to wages. A second suggestion is to raise the normal retirement age to 68. The 1983 Social Security Amendments will eventually raise the age to 67, but the transition is not complete until 2027. If the system is fully adopted to conform to private insurance principles, as described above, these two changes would be rendered unnecessary.

For tactical reasons, Ferrara also recommends that Social Security financing be shifted from the payroll tax to the federal general fund. This is not a necessary feature of his phase-out plan, but he speculates that it would help rein in all federal programs by forcing Social Security to compete with other expenditures. It would also intensify pressure for a means test for the welfare component.

Proposed long-term reforms are designed to shift the insurance function of Social Security to the private sector. This could be accomplished through the following steps.

1. Abolish the payroll tax and stop the accrual of additional benefit obligations.

2. Allow private insurers to apply to the government for certification as purveyors of retirement, disability, and perhaps hospital insurance. Firms would be required to demonstrate sound management of funds, to

avoid investments with undue risk, and to abide by traditional insurance principles. Investments would be guaranteed by the government.

3. Calculate the age at which individuals can get higher returns from private investments than from Social Security. This age might be 35, but could be older if private investments are given additional tax breaks. Persons at or below the cutoff age would be required to invest a certain percentage of their earnings in retirement funds. The percentage could equal previous Social Security tax rates, but they might be less given the higher rate of return to private savings. The annual payment requirement could be made flexible, subject to a minimum lifetime constraint, to accommodate variable demand for savings over the life cycle.

4. Divide the workforce into three age categories. Those under the cutoff age described above (assumed to be 40) would be given a choice. They could remain in Social Security, pay taxes as before, and be given bonds equal in value to past taxes plus an inflation adjustment, or they could invest the required amount in prescribed private retirement funds. Those who opt out of Social Security forfeit any claim to benefits earned *prior* to the introduction of the private option. This forfeiture applies whether they opt out immediately or at a later date. Because returns to the private alternative are expected to be higher, Ferrara anticipates that most younger workers will opt out.

Workers age 40 to 60 at the time of transition could not be expected to gain enough from private savings to compensate fully for loss of Social Security. These individuals would be offered two options. They could invest an amount equal to previous Social Security tax payments in private retirement accounts. In addition they would be issued bonds scheduled to mature at retirement that would give them an amount equal to the value of promised Social Security benefits minus expected returns from their private retirement accounts. If the private accounts perform as expected they will be no better or worse off than under Social Security. Alternatively, they could continue to pay Social Security taxes for the purchase of bonds that would return at retirement an amount equal to taxes plus an inflation adjustment. Since private retirement accounts are expected to earn positive real returns, this would appear to be an unattractive alternative. For persons remaining in Social Security, similar arrangements would apply to survivors and disability insurance, i.e., benefits would be based on previous contributions adjusted for inflation.

Persons age 60 and over at time of transition would receive all of the benefits to which they are currently entitled. These persons as well as those already in beneficiary status would be unaffected by the change.

Because payroll taxes would no longer be available to pay beneficiaries, any transitional costs would be covered out of federal general funds. This would be a large amount initially, but as persons over age 60 at the time of transition die off, the payments would drop off rapidly. Within 30 years, the costs would be negligible. Current federal deficits are much larger than when Ferrara first published his phase-out plan. Consequently, opposition to the transition would now be much stronger. In recognition of this consideration, he has formulated a more modest phase-out proposal that would create much less of a drain on the general fund. Of course it would also take longer to complete the phase-out.[25]

The 1985 Version

The new proposal contains two major features. First, it would secure the benefits of the elderly by creating a contractual obligation guaranteeing them monthly benefits plus cost-of-living adjustments for life. Those already retired would acquire the same protection as holders of government bonds. They would not feel threatened by changes affecting the working population.

Persons still working would be offered what Ferrara calls a "Super IRA." They would be allowed to contribute up to 20 percent of their current payroll tax liability to an individual retirement account, to be matched by an equal contribution out of the employer's liability. Payroll taxes would not be reduced, since the revenue is needed to cover current benefit payments. Instead, workers and employers would receive a 100 percent income tax credit for contributions to the Super IRA. This is more attractive than an IRA deduction, which cuts tax liability only by the taxpayer's marginal income tax rate.[26] For persons exercising the IRA option, future Social Security benefits would be reduced by a formula that reflects both the amount invested and period of participation in the IRA option. As an example, a worker who allocated 20 percent of payroll tax liability to an IRA over the entire working career would experience a 20 percent reduction in benefits. Because returns to the IRA are expected to exceed returns to Social Security, the IRA option would be attractive.

Additional credit options could be added to allow the purchase of life or disability insurance. This would enable workers to substitute private life and disability insurance for SI and DI. Private insurers might also offer health insurance that could be purchased by workers in advance to go into effect after retirement.

The upper limit on the share of payroll tax allocated to the Super IRA, along with the income tax credit, could gradually be increased, eventually reaching 100 percent. As IRAs replace Social Security the system would slowly be phased down, eliminating its long-term financing problems.

Because the payroll tax would continue, the initial cost to the general fund would be much less than under Ferrara's 1980 plan. Ferrara estimates a cost of about $14 billion per year with the 20 percent credit on retirement accounts. The cost would rise over time, but Ferrara expects this to be offset by the extra burst of economic growth that would be induced by the phasing down of Social Security.[27]

Once the phase-out is complete, via whichever arrangement, Ferrara foresees a withdrawal of government from direct control over saving for retirement and the purchase of insurance. He appears to favor continuation of tax shelters for retirement saving, however, because of the boost it would give to capital formation and economic growth.

Preview

The essays that follow examine some of the major issues raised by those who favor a phase-out of Social Security. Returns to Social Security are said to be far below returns to private retirement accounts. Bruno Stein's essay on the Ferrara proposal presents data on real rates of return to private pension portfolios and examines the prospects for future reliance on this income source. The issue of comparative returns has crucial implications for the political prospects for a phase-out. Ferrara and others emphasize the low returns to payroll taxes that are projected for persons currently working, especially for persons born after 1945. They also point to inequities in the distribution of benefits within retirement cohorts. These issues are examined in the essay by Charles W. Meyer and Nancy L. Wolff on intracohort and intercohort redistribution.

Generations in the workforce during a phase-out must absorb the cost of providing benefits to retired workers while also contributing to retirement funds for their own retirement. Ferrara claims that the burst of saving and capital formation that will accompany a phase-out will make the transition self-financing. This is because Social Security displaces retirement saving and lowers the overall rate of saving in the economy. The essay by Selig D. Lesnoy and Dean R. Leimer on Social Security and private saving examines the evidence that supports this claim.

Social Security is alleged to have undesirable effects on the functioning of the labor market. In particular, it encourages early retirement. As a consequence, elderly Americans lose earnings as well as additional retirement savings that they would accumulate in the absence of Social Security. Rachel F. Boaz writes about the labor market behavior of workers approaching retirement and examines empirical evidence relating to the labor supply of older workers. She also looks at demand for the labor of older workers and discusses the extent to which weak demand is responsible for early retirement.

In the concluding essay, Meyer examines the market-failure arguments for compulsory social insurance and concludes with a critique of Ferrara's plan for a phase-out. The effect of a phase-out on the economy and the prospects for political support for radical reform are evaluated.

Notes

1. In 1986 a worker received one quarter of coverage for each $440 of covered annual earnings. No more than four quarters can be credited for each year. The amount of earnings needed to get a quarter of coverage increases automatically each year to keep pace with average earnings.

2. At the rate of 50 cents on the dollar, the benefit reduction applies to annual earnings in the range between the exemption level and twice the annual benefit. Above the upper limit benefits cease. When the benefit reduction falls to $1 for every $3 of earnings the marginal "tax" rate will fall accordingly, but the upper limit on affected earnings will rise to the exemption level plus three times annual benefits.

3. Weaver (1982), p. 9.

4. Weaver (1982), p. 37.

5. Weaver (1982), pp. 72–76.

6. Cates (1983), pp. 24–40.

7. Cates (1983), pp. 19–20; Weaver (1982), p. 71.

8. Weaver (1982), p. 123.

9. The expansion of Social Security between 1969 and 1973 is described in detail in Derthick (1979), pp. 339–368.

10. A detailed summary of the report of the National Commission, the legislative history of the 1983 amendments, and a description and analysis of the provisions of the 1983 Social Security amendments are found in Svahn and Ross (1983).

11. Projections for HI and OASDI trust funds are found in U.S. Congress, Committee on Ways and Means (1985a, b).

12. Robertson (1983), p. 407.

13. Campbell (1969).

14. Ferrara (1980), pp. 252–253.

15. Ferrara (1985), p. 2.

16. For a description of several proposals for radical reform of Social Security, see Ferrara (1980), pp. 311–350.

17. Martin Feldstein (1975) has proposed that Social Security be retained but gradually transformed into a funded system. His goal is to increase aggregate saving and investment.

18. Ferrara's original version of a phase-out plan appears in Ferrara (1980), pp. 371–391. Proposals for a more gradual phase-out appear in Ferrara (1982), pp. 101–128 and Ferrara (1985), pp. 193–213.

19. Ferrara (1980), p. 284.

20. Ferrara (1980), pp. 163–165.

21. Pilon (1983), p. 604.

22. Ferrara (1985), p. 186.

23. Ferrara (1985), pp. 178–183.

24. Ferrara (1980), pp. 371–391.
25. Ferrara (1985), pp. 193–220.
26. Ferrara (1985), pp. 194–195.
27. Ferrara (1985), pp. 197–198.

Bibliography

Campbell, C.D. (1969). "Social Insurance in the United States: A Program in Search of an Explanation." *Journal of Law and Economics* (12), October, pp. 249–265.

Cates, J.R. (1983). *Insuring Inequality* (Ann Arbor: University of Michigan Press).

Derthick, D. (1979). *Policy Making for Social Security* (Washington, DC: The Brookings Institution).

Feldstein, M.S. (1975). "Toward a Reform of Social Security," *Public Interest* (401), Summer, pp. 75–95.

Ferrara, P.J. (1980). *Social Security: The Inherent Contradiction* (San Francisco: Cato Institute).

———. (1982). *Social Security: Averting the Crisis* (Washington, DC: Cato Institute).

———. ed., (1985). *Social Security: Prospects for Real Reform* (Washington, DC: Cato Institute).

Pilon, R. (1983). "Beyond Efficiency: A Comment," *Cato Journal* (3), Fall, pp. 603–608.

Robertson, A.H. (1983). "The National Commission's Failure to Achieve Real Reform," *Cato Journal* (3), Fall, pp. 403–416.

Svahn, J.A. and M. Ross. (1983). Social Security Amendments of 1983: Legislative History and Summary of Provisions, *Social Security Bulletin* (46), July, pp. 3–48.

U.S. Congress, House Committee on Ways and Means. (1986a). *1986 Annual Report of the Board of Trustees of the Federal Hospital Insurance Trust Fund*, 99th Congress, 1st Session, April 1.

———. (1986b). *1986 Annual Report of the Board of Trustees of the Federal Old-Age and Survivors Insurance and Disability Insurance Trust Funds*, 99th Congress, 1st Session, April 1.

Weaver, C.L. (1982). *The Crisis in Social Security* (Durham, NC: Duke Press Policy Studies).

2
Phasing Out Social Security: A Critique of Ferrara's Proposal

Bruno Stein

S ocial Security has been in trouble. Beginning in the mid-1970s, the system displayed alarming symptoms of malfunctioning. It was under-financed, which means that its revenues were falling short of its obligations or, if you prefer, its obligations were too great for its promises of benefit. On the legislative scene, this led to considerable tearing of hair and gnashing of teeth as policy makers tried to cope with one of the hotter problems on the political horizon. It is deservedly hot because Americans, like the citizens of all industrial states, have come to depend on Social Security as a nonmeans-tested—and therefore dignified—form of income maintenance available against the contingencies of old age, disability, premature death of a parent, and health care in old age. They have thought of it as *secure,* and have built their plans around its existence.

The problems have not been solely financial. Social Security is rife with inequalities, malfunctions, distortions, disincentives, and redistributions that are not to everyone's taste, and in some cases, positively bizarre.[1] It is note-worthy, however, that these dysfunctions were not what was capturing the popular imagination in the recent crisis. Most Americans are concerned with the security of Social Security, and most legislative efforts were directed toward fixing the machinery rather than scrapping it. Whether these efforts will succeed or fail in the long run remains to be seen. Social Security's cash transfer system was "fixed" in 1972, 1977, and 1981, and it received a major overhaul in 1983.[2]

When a device is in continuous need of repair, there is an obvious temp-tation to consider scrapping it and acquiring a new one. This is precisely what Ferrara proposes to do.[3] He is not the first critic to suggest this. Other proposals to phase out public Social Security have been made by such econ-omists as Laffer and Ranson, Buchanan, and Friedman.[4] In this paper I shall focus on Ferrara, who has gone further than others in an attempt to show how the insurance goals of Social Security can be achieved in the context of the private sector market for insurance and annuities. In view of the current resurgence of preference for private sector over public sector solutions, his well thought-out proposal is worthy of consideration.

Since it is difficult to consider a social policy like Social Security without reference to normative values, it should be noted that Ferrara is frank in stating his prejudices: he is a libertarian. My own views are more eclectic, and my purpose is neither to bury Social Security nor to praise it. However, I find it difficult to envision a capitalist industrial society without *some* social insurance provisions and other social policies. To me, a necessary (but not always sufficient) condition for judging a social policy is whether it is workable within the limits of commonly acceptable moral and institutional constraints.[5] Therefore, I shall focus on the workability of the Ferrara proposal.

The plan of my paper is, as follows. I shall begin by examining the inherent contradiction which, according to Ferrara, conceptually undermines Social Security. I shall then touch upon the conservative bases of social insurance systems and their possibilities for adaption to adverse conditions. Next, I shall look at the economic (rather than social or political) bases of the Ferrara proposal. Thereafter, I shall present what little data is available on the historical performance of private pensions and similar funds. This is necessary because Ferrara's plan is based on future projections of performance that appear to be overly optimistic. I shall conclude that the proposal to privatize Social Security rests on shaky theoretical and empirical foundations.

The Inherent Contradiction

A central thesis of Ferrara's work is that social insurance is a mix of insurance and welfare. An insurance program pays benefits on the occurrence of the insured-against contingency: the size of the benefit is a function of the premiums and has no relation to need. A welfare program, *per contra,* pays benefits to persons in need, and the amount of the benefits is based on need rather than on previous contributions to the program. While this is not strictly true,[6] it will do for a good approximation of the contrast between private and social insurance. The result of this mix of functions is said to be bad insurance and bad welfare.

The point is important and needs to be explored. The two functions are certainly separable, and Munnell (among others) has suggested that they be separated.[7] A pure welfare program can be more target-efficient, but it should be noted that welfare programs are costly to administer and create their own disincentives, not to mention moral hazard. Moreover, shifting the welfare function of Social Security to supplemental security income (SSI) and other pure welfare programs is not cost-free. It may relieve some burden on Social Security, but creates one for the rest of the fisc. To the extent that such programs receive revenues from regressive state taxes, they do not provide relief from the problem that poor people are taxed to pay benefits to other poor people.

Social insurance and public assistance programs complement one another, since the latter exist to take care of those who lack sufficient coverage to make do with social insurance and who have no other resources. Those who wish to shift completely from social to private old age insurance have some obligation to tell us something about the parallel "welfare" system that would be needed under these circumstances. In Ferrara, and in many others like him, this detail is lacking. There are references to SSI and an assertion that a removal of the welfare function from Social Security would not necessarily increase SSI expenditures. Perhaps not, but this is an empirical question. Moreover, a libertarian would want to propose a public assistance system that maximizes individual liberty. Welfare systems, by their nature, are coercive, a point recognized by Friedman when he proposed his negative income tax. One reason for putting some welfare functions into Social Security was to reduce the amount of coercion to which the marginally poor are exposed.

Part of the issue is semantic. Social insurance is simply not the same thing as private insurance. The word insurance, in this context, is a misnomer. It has a mythic content, and may well have been chosen to mislead, as Ferrara believes; however, it is used throughout the world and was not invented in the United States. If we use the word in a sense parallel to private insurance, we must be careful to define what contingencies are insured against. For example, old age insurance (OAI) is not an annuity. The insured contingency is loss of labor earnings from old age. In this context, the retirement test makes sense. If you are old but working, the contingency has not occurred; if my house does not burn down, I cannot claim fire insurance benefits either. Seen in this light, the inequity lies not in the inability of workers to collect an annuity at age 65 if their labor earnings are too great; it lies in the actuarially unfair retirement credit for work past age 65.[8] It may be noted that some occupational pensions contain a similar inequity in not counting service beyond the pension plan's normal retirement age.[9]

Welfare States and Industrial Societies

All industrial societies have social insurance systems of one sort or another. Our system is among the least developed. Social insurance systems did not originate during the Great Depression; they are phenomena that date back to the end of the nineteenth century and were responses to the political instability that is consequent upon the economic instability inherent in market economies. In this sense, they were conservative, not radical. Their begettors were Tories, not Whigs or Socialists. Bismarck, who helped to found the world's first comprehensive social insurance system, was neither noted for his compassion nor for his devotion to democracy.[10] It is an error to suppose that the enrichment of social insurance provisions is nothing more than an exercise in vote buying. It may lend itself to that purpose in democratic societies, and politicians have been known to succumb to this temptation.[11] However, retrenchment is also possible. In Britain the Thatcher regime has reduced some benefits. In the United States, the 1983 amendments led to some thinly disguised cuts in benefits. The democratic process has some capability for adjusting to perceived social needs in both directions.

In short, it is no coincidence that industrial societies developed social insurance programs, nor is it a coincidence that, faced with problems similar to ours, they may move toward the reduction of social welfare programs that, in retrospect, may have proved to be overambitious. Social forces can be more powerful than ideology.

The Economic Bases of Ferrara's Program

Ferrara contends that the private sector can outperform Social Security in providing for the contingencies covered by Social Security. He is undoubtedly correct in pointing out that Social Security is no longer as good a "buy" for the incoming cohort of workers as it was for prior generations. The start-up effect of the pay-as-you-go system is ending and the gift given to earlier generations must be paid for. Declining rates of economic growth have caused the resource base to rise less rapidly than in earlier decades. Finally, and most excruciatingly, the ratio of retirees to workers will be rising because of unfavorable demographic trends. As this process works itself out, the intergenerational transfer component of Social Security benefits declines and may, in time, become negative.[12] The 1983 amendments do not prevent a declining rate of return to younger cohorts.

One way or another, a small cohort of workers will have to support a large cohort of pensioners. The argument that private markets will do a superior job rests on three propositions, all of which are questionable, at least for the time being. They are:

1. The hypothesis that Social Security depresses savings and capital formation, thus inhibiting economic growth; this is based on the work of Feldstein and is grounded on the life-cycle theory of saving and consumption behavior.[13]
2. The evolving theory of supply-side economics.
3. The ability of pension portfolio managers to capture high real rates of return.

The Feldstein Hypothesis

Feldstein's studies on the depressing effect of Social Security on savings have attracted considerable attention. The notion that old age (and other) benefits displace saving and retard capital formation is a plausible one. Nevertheless, the issue is far from settled. There are equally plausible critiques from Barro, Darby, and Munnell. Lesnoy and Leimer discovered a programming error in Feldstein's econometrics that further undermined its plausibility.[14] At all times, however, the Feldstein hypothesis must contend with the facts that (1) the ratio of personal saving to disposable income has not declined in the United States since the advent of Social Security and (2) that people retiring today have saved about the same proportion of income as those who retired thirty years ago.[15] Studies made in Canada, Germany, Britain, France, and Sweden show no evidence in the first four of these countries of any depressing effects of social security programs on saving. The exception is Sweden, but there the program is heavily funded, and the reduction in saving has been more than offset by growth in fund assets.[16]

It is possible, moreover, that life cycle theory, which is the basis for Feldstein's model, may not be an adequate theory of lifetime saving and spending behavior. This idea has been suggested by Mordecai Kurz. Using a cross-sectional analysis, he concludes that the life cycle hypothesis "should not be regarded as providing a significant scientific basis for the explanation of the process of capital accumulation in our society." He finds that the displacement effect of Social Security on wealth accumulation ranges from the small to trivial except in the case of single males. This, he admits, leaves us with no coherent theory of family saving.[17] I suggest that it may be better to admit what we do not know than to rely on the doubtful. Henry Aaron's analysis arrives at similar conclusions.[18] Feldstein may or may not be right; he may turn out to be right, for all I know, but one should hesitate to base a radical policy proposal on a proposition that is in such great dispute.

The Supply-Side Effect

The Ferrara plan creates a universal tax shelter and adds some new tax shelters on top of the existing ones. Common sense tells us that everyone cannot be sheltered. Somebody has to pay taxes if we are to have the services of government. The massive tax reductions that Ferrara implies must be made up in some fashion, and we may find that his plan leads to tax increases that offset his tax cuts. I do not think that I gain anything if, *ceteris paribus,* you cut my taxes by $10 annually and raise them by $10 annually at the same time.

It is possible, of course, that the supply-side effect of Ferrara's universal tax shelter is so powerful that no tax increase will be needed to make up for the revenue shortfall. At this stage in the development of economics, the supply-side effect is not something on which many economists would care to rely. This includes some persons formerly in the Reagan administration, including Martin Feldstein and former Budget Director David Stockman.[19] The supply-side experiment in existence since the 1981 tax cuts has led to mixed results, at best, and it may be wise to await a stronger outcome before using the theory to scuttle Social Security.

A further note on the tax sheltering of retirement saving: Ferrara proposes to shelter enterprises from corporate income taxes to the extent that their shares are owned by pension funds. Ferrara is, of course, looking for a mechanism that passes the pre-tax rate of return on capital through to retirement savers. The proposal would, however, create some interesting distortions into capital markets. If pension fund portfolio managers prefer stodgy low risk securities, as they might (being prudent persons), then such enterprises will pay lower taxes. Their shares will rise in price and offset the risk premiums available to high risk investors. That may not be a good thing for a dynamic economy and may lead to a sort of negative supply-side effect.

Pension Funds and Real Rates of Return

There is many a slip 'twixt the cup and the lip.' Historical real-after-tax rates of return on capital may well be in the ranges of 6 to 8 percent that Ferrara indicates, but two problems must be faced: (1) history is a record of the past, not of the future, and (2) soundly managed portfolios rarely capture average historical rates of return.

Nordhaus has estimated the "genuine" rate of return of nonfinancial corporate capital through time, and finds that it has been falling.[20] Feldstein and Summers have taken him to task for assuming that the low rates of the 1970s are more than temporary, and give evidence to the contrary.[21] I hope that Feldstein and Summers are right, since a falling rate of profit portends evil for many other things, including Social Security. Be that as it may, Nordhaus' "genuine" before-tax rate for the period 1948–1979 averages 12.4 percent.[22] This puts it into the same order of magnitude as Holland and Meyers' estimate of a real pre-tax rate of 12.6 percent for nonfinancial corporations.[23] After-tax returns are, of course, a little more than half of this, say between 6 and 7 percent, depending on effective corporate income tax rates.

So far, so good. Undoubtedly, there are shrewd investors who do as well, or better. There are others who do much worse. Professional portfolio managers are probably among the latter, the more so when prudence is called for, as in the case of pension funds. In any event, differences in rates of return to pension funds can be enormous in any given year—as high as twenty percentage points on equities—which shows that portfolio management is a highly imperfect art.[24]

Historical Evidence

Complete long-term data on the performance of pension funds are nonexistent. It may be useful, therefore, to begin with a hypothetical example for a fifty year period, 1930–1980. Assume that pension funds, had they been in existence that long (and very few have this long a history) had asembled equity portfolios consisting of all of the stocks in the Standard and Poor 500 Index and debt portfolios consisting of all of the securities in the Salomon Brothers Bond Index. I use these data because they are available for so long a time period, even though "index funds" have only recently come into being.

Abstracting from transaction costs, and from the near-impossibly for any smaller fund of acquiring such portfolios, the real rates of return are shown in table 2–1.

A portfolio balanced at a prudent but not entirely risk-averse ratio of 65 percent equity and 35 percent bonds would have yielded a real rate of 3.15 percent. Other mixes would have given different results. The maximum possibility would have been 4.9 percent, which approaches the rates envisioned by Ferrara. However, a portfolio consisting entirely of equity would have been considered imprudent for a pension fund even before the advent of ERISA. Accordingly, returns approximating a real rate of 5 percent would not have been achieved.

One fund with long term data that are publicly available is (Teachers Insurance and Annuity Association—College Retirement Equities Fund) TIAA-CREF. This is the largest fund in existence, and CREF tracks the S&P 500 pretty well. The period 1952–1980 covers most of the growth and maturation of pension funds in the United States. The performance of TIAA and CREF during this time is given in table 2–2.

Table 2–1
Real Rates of Return, 1930–1980
(CPI as inflation measure)

Standard & Poor 500	4.9%
Salomon Brothers Bond Index	−0.1%

Source: Courtesy of Peat, Marwick, Mitchell, and Company.

Table 2–2
**Real Rates of Return to TIAA and CREF,
1952–1980**
(CPI as inflation measure)

CREF	4.8%
TIAA	1.6%

Source: CREF rate computed from TIAA-CREF (1980), Part A. TIAA rate computed from 1960–1980 data in TIAA-CREF (1980) and for 1952 to 1959 from data provided by TIAA.

As table 2–2 shows, the real rate of return on CREF was 4.8 percent. Many policy holders divided their contributions on the 50-50 basis. This gave a real return of 3.2 percent, which is far from the 5 to 8 percent range projected by Ferrara. The less risk-averse policy holders who chose 75 percent CREF and 25 percent TIAA managed a swinging real rate of 4 percent. Obviously, individual experience varies with dates of entry and retirement, as well as with individual tastes for risk. Even with a knowledge of modern portfolio theory, savers who earmark part of their saving for retirement and are given choices of varying degree of risk (as is the case with TIAA-CREF) are, in most cases, unlikely to take the riskiest option for this purpose.

Data for shorter time periods are more available, but less useful for our purpose. Still they can be instructive. Median performance of pension funds tracked by A.G. Becker and Co. are shown in table 2–3. It should be remembered that fifteen years is not a short time in the life of a pension fund if you consider that most *lifetime* employees have a maximum work-life expectancy of about forty-five years.

A point often overlooked in the discussions of rates of return to private pension funds is their considerable volatility from year to year. This is especially true of funds invested in equities. For example, funds tracked by A.G. Becker showed a median nominal rate of − 31.6 percent in 1974, followed in 1975 by a positive nominal rate of 33.1 percent.[25] A number of bad years in succession can raise the specter of underfunding among funds that are weak in the first place. The obverse is that a number of good years lead to overfunding. Although good years and bad years should average out over the long haul, overfunding creates a temptation to employers to terminate a defined benefit fund, recapture the excess and (if they choose), start a new fund, usually of the defined contribution type. Overfunding calculations do not take into consideration the possibility of future inflation. In real terms, an overfunded pension fund might not have any excess assets. Hence, the maneuver can deprive covered employees of some future inflation protection in addition to shifting investment risks from employers to workers.

Table 2–3
Median Real Rates of Return on A.G.
Becker-tracked Funds, 1965–1980
(CPI as inflation measure)

Equity	−1.37%
Debt	−2.47%
Total Fund	−1.77%

Source: Courtesy of Peat, Marwick, Mitchell, and Company.

This process has begun to pick up some speed in the 1980s, as rising stock and bond markets created overfunding in actuarial terms. Between January 1980 and the end of June 1985, some 536 plans, covering 637,402 participants, were terminated. Close to $5 billion in assets were recaptured. Pending at that time were another 216 terminations, covering 271,281 participants, with the goal of recapturing $2.7 billion in assets.[26] In short, private pensions have the interesting property of being able to defeat employee expectation both in bad times and in good times.

Indexation of Pension Funds

Indexation to the CPI is rare in the private sector pension funds, notwithstanding Ferrara's belief that sellers of annuities would be willing to guarantee inflation-proofing of benefits. Of 216 conventional, i.e., non-bargained, plans surveyed by Bankers Trust Co. for the period from 1975 to 1980, only nine (4.2 percent) reported annual adjustments triggered by and related to changes in the CPI. All had "caps" ranging from 2.5 percent to 4 percent. Pattern plans (collectively bargained) reported no automatic adjustments. It may be noteworthy that six of the nine plans with automatic adjustments covered insurance company employees.

Over the same five year period, 153 conventional plans and 44 pattern plans reported ad hoc adjustments. In the conventional plans, most (66 percent) had made only one adjustment, whereas the frequency of adjustment was greater in the pattern plans.[27]

Full inflation proofing is simply not possible for funded plans in a world of unanticipated inflation. Nominal interest rates may track price level changes in the long run, but annuity payments are made monthly and portfolios can only be adjusted at the margin.

However, it is possible to devise annuities whose payments vary somewhat with inflation, on the theory that current nominal interest rates consist of a basic rate plus an inflation premium. TIAA-CREF's graded benefit payment method offers the option of a lower basic annuity, with the difference between the lower base and the full annuity being credited to the annuitant and earning current interest rates. This permits benefits to rise through time if higher prices lead to higher interest rates.[28] This, in reality, is inflation insurance, in which much of the risk is borne by the annuitant, and it takes advantage of the tax-free status of earnings that have been credited but not yet paid out.

It is always possible that some other funds might offer such inflation insurance. On the other hand, if the movement to recapture the "excess" assets of defined benefit funds becomes a regular pro-cyclical activity, inflation protection for those funds is diminished. It would seem from the above that the inflation-proofing that is inherent in proposals of the Ferrara type is a chimera.

Where Do We Go from Here?

There is not the slightest doubt that Social Security remains in a period of transition. The most pressing reason for the changes that can be anticipated is that the system (even after the 1983 amendments) may lead to some acute intergenerational strains. Moreover, one cannot really rely on 75-year projections of actuarial balance. The system also needs to adapt itself to changes in family structure and the changing role of women in the labor market. However, the last item still appears to have a lower political priority than the first two even though it is fraught with many of the inequities that Ferrara and others have found.

The system that will emerge is likely to be a leaner one. The 1977 amendments slowed the rise in real benefits to increases in average wages and, indeed lowered them in terms of replacement ratios. Further reductions were made in 1983. If this is the case, then some substitution of private retirement savings for Social Security may occur. This can take many forms. Households may adjust their savings behavior, although this is not evident as of 1986. Employers may offer more in pensions relative to cash wages. If unions regain their strength, they may demand more in pensions, presumably at the expense of cash or other benefits. Government policies to induce or even coerce retirement saving may be developed.[29] Closer integration of private and public retirement programs may lead us closer to a full funding of the sum total of our retirement income obligations.[30]

If this is the case, then the direction of change is toward Ferrara's goal of greater reliance on private savings and less on pay-as-you-go public schemes. This may be all to the good in terms of future capital formation and possibly, in terms of the functioning of a market economy. It may bring us closer to the ideals of the founders of Social Security, who envisioned it only as a foundation on which households would accumulate private assets.

Conclusion

I have, in this paper, tried to show that Ferrara's program may not be workable. Its theoretical underpinnings are debatable and, as a practical matter, the possibility of achieving the real rates of return to pension investments that he forecasts are highly unlikely. If I am right, then there is no point in my discussing the proposals to phase in the plan. One would not want to phase in a social policy unless one had more confidence in the outcome, since the potential for serious mischief is not inconsiderable.

Under the circumstances, a retirement system with some redistributive features is likely to remain a part of the scene in advanced capitalist economies like ours. After all, someone has got to support the old folks, including the poor ones. That support will be costly as our nation enters the twenty-first century, largely because of the declining ratio of economically active to inactive elderly persons. This may be unfair to the small cohort workers who will need to help the large cohort of pensioners. Solving this problem will require more than faith in life cycle theory or ideological preferences for a libertarian world.

The value of Ferrara's work is that it draws our attention to the need for reform. It does this dramatically, and forces us to rethink what we once took for granted, and to face a reality that is painful: In my world—albeit a second best world—this is a high compliment.

Notes

1. Many of these are summarized in Stein (1980).

2. For some proposals to repair the system, see National Commission on Social Security (1981) and President's Commission on Pension Policy (1981). An analysis of both proposals is found in Stein (1981). An analysis of the 1983 amendment is found in Stein (1984).

3. See Ferrara (1980) and Ferrara (1985).

4. See Laffer and Ranson (1977), Buchanan (1968), and Friedman (1962). Also see Friedman's discussion in Cohen and Friedman (1972) and the various proposals summarized in Ferrara (1980), pp. 311–350.

5. The constraints *are* important. To take a polar extreme, a nation's racial or ethnic conflicts can be solved by eliminating one or the other parties to the conflict. This violates the moral values of most of us, but it clearly did not trouble the National Socialist German Workers' Party.

6. I can insure my $100 watch for $1,000 against the contingency of theft, but the insurance company will only pay me $100 if the watch is stolen, even though my premiums were based on a $1,000 policy. Similarly, many welfare programs do not pay on exact need, but classify claimants by presumed need.

7. Munnell (1977), pp. 39–40, 92–93.

8. There are, however, other valid arguments against the retirement test, based on the withdrawal of labor that it induces. The 1983 amendments phase in a fairer actuarial adjustment for work past the retirement age.

9. While we are at it, we may note that some private occupational pensions also contain "inequitable" redistributive features, not the least being past service credits for newly covered workers. However, the Employees Retirement Income Security Act (ERISA) requires that these be amortized over a thirty-year period. As of 1986, there are proposals to require employers to maintain pension contributions past age 65.

10. For a discussion of the development of social insurance, with reference to Bismarck's motives, see Stein (1980), pp. 34–38.

11. Anecdotal evidence has it that the benefit increases of the 1972 Social Security amendments were tribute to the presidential ambitions of Congressman Wilbur Mills. For a discussion of this, see Derthick (1979), pp. 358–362.

12. See Parsons and Munro (1977), pp. 69–86.

13. The original and classic version is Feldstein (1974).

14. See Barro (1977), Darby (1978), Munnell (1974a, b), and Leimer and Lesnoy (1982). For an excellent critique of the Feldstein hypothesis, see Aaron (1982), pp. 40–52.

15. See Munnell (1981), pp. 40–42.

16. See von Furstenberg (1979), chapters 5–8. However, von Furstenberg concludes that "there is some agreement [in the studies] that social security wealth or the associated taxes will reduce private saving in the future." See p. 13.

17. See Mordecai Kurz (1981).

18. See Aaron (1982), pp. 12–23.

19. See Stockman (1986).

20. See Nordhaus (1974), pp. 169–208. The "genuine" rate cleans up for inventory valuation adjustments and capital consumption allowances.

21. See Feldstein and Summers (1977), pp. 211–227.

22. Computed from data for 1948–54 in Nordhaus (1974), p. 180 and for 1955–79 from U.S. president (1982), p. 331. The merging of these two data sources results in a slight upward bias, since the latter series appears to have some downward revisions for overlapping years.

23. See Holland and Meyers (1980), p. 321.

24. See Kotlikoff and Smith (1983), pp. 337–351.

25. See Kotlikoff and Smith (1983), pp. 337–351.

26. See Asinof (1985). The data in the article were supplied by the Pension Benefit Guarantee Corporation. Also see Bernheim and Shoven (1985), pp. 5–13. As of June 1986, a legislative proposal in the Senate would levy a 10 percent tax on recaptured assets.

27. Cited in King (1981).

28. See TIAA-CREF (1981).

29. The President's Commission on Pension Policy (1981) recommended a minimum universal pension system (MUPS) on top of a somewhat reduced Social Security system. In 1981 Congress liberalized provisions for individual retirement accounts, but legislation pending in 1986 may reverse this policy.

30. George M. von Furstenberg makes a useful distinction between funding in the accounting sense and in the economic sense. He notes that Canada and Sweden, despite very different retirement policies, are closer to full funding in the economic sense than we are. See von Furstenberg (1979), pp. 3–21.

Bibliography

Aaron, H.J. (1982). *Economic Effects of Social Security* (Washington, DC: The Brookings Institution).

Asinof, L. (1985). "Excess Pension Assets Lure Corporate Raiders," *Wall Street Journal,* September 11, p. 6.

Barro, R.J. (1977). "Social Security and Private Saving: Evidence from U.S. Time Series," University of Rochester (processed), April.

Bernheim, B.D. and J.B. Shoven. (1985). "Pension Funding and Saving," National Bureau of Economic Research Working Paper No. 1622, May.

Buchanan, J.M. (1968). "Social Security in a Growing Economy: A Proposal for Radical Reform," *National Tax Journal* (21), December, pp. 386–395.

Cohen, W.J. and M. Friedman. (1972). *Social Security: Universal or Selective?* (Washington, DC: American Enterprise Institute).

Darby, M.R. (1979). *The Effects of Social Security on Income and the Capital Stock* (Washington, DC: American Enterprise Institute).

Derthick, M. (1979). *Policymaking for Social Security* (Washington, DC: The Brookings Institution).

Feldstein, M.S. (1974). "Social Security, Induced Retirement, and Aggregate Capital Formation," *Journal of Political Economy* (82), September/October, pp. 905–925.

—— and L. Summers. (1977). "Is the Rate of Profit Falling?" *Brookings Papers on Economic Activity* I, pp. 211–227.

Ferrara, P.J. (1980). *Social Security: The Inherent Contradiction* (San Francisco: Cato Institute).

——. (1985) *Social Security: Prospects for Real Reform* (Washington, DC: Cato Institute).

Friedman, M. (1962). *Capitalism and Freedom* (Chicago: University of Chicago Press).

Holland, D.M. and S.C. Meyers. (1980). "Profitability and Capital Costs for Manufacturing Corporations and All Nonfinancial Corporations," *American Economic Review* 70 (May), pp. 320–325.

King, F.P. (1981). "Indexing Retirement Benefits," prepared for meeting of the Gerontological Society of America, November 8.

Kotlikoff, L.J. and D.E. Smith. (1983). *Pensions in the American Economy* (Chicago: University of Chicago Press).

Kurz, M. (1981). "Effects of Social Security and Private Pensions on Family Savings," SRI International (processed), April.

Laffer, A.B. and R.D. Ranson. (1977). "A Proposal for Reforming Social Security," (Boston: H.C. Wainright & Co.), May 19.

Leimer, D.R. and S.D. Lesnoy. (1982). "Social Security and Private Saving: New Time Series Evidence," *Journal of Political Economy* (90), June, pp. 606–642.

Munnell, A.H. (1974a). *The Effect of Social Security on Personal Savings* (Cambridge, MA: Ballinger).

——. (1974b). "The Impact of Social Security on Personal Savings," *National Tax Journal* (27), December, pp. 553–567.

——. (1977). *The Future of Social Security* (Washington, DC: The Brookings Institution).

——. (1981). "Social Security, Private Pensions, and Saving," *New England Economic Review,* May/June, pp. 31–47.

National Commission on Social Security. (1981). *Social Security in America's Future: Final Report* (Washington, DC), March 12.

Nordhaus, W.D. (1974). "The Falling Share of Profits," *Brookings Papers on Economic Activity* III, pp. 169–208.

Parsons, D.O. and D.R. Munro. (1977). "Intergenerational Transfers in Social Security," in M.J. Boskin, ed., *The Crisis in Social Security: Problems and Prospects* (San Francisco: Institute for Contemporary Studies), pp. 69–86.

President's Commission on Pension Policy. (1981). *Coming of Age: Toward a National Retirement Income Policy* (Washington, DC), February 20.

Stein, B. (1980). *Social Security and Pensions in Transition: Understanding the American Retirement System* (New York: Free Press/Macmillan).

———. (1981). "Changing the American Retirement System," in D.L. Salisbury, ed., *Retirement Income and the Economy* (Washington, DC: Employee Benefit Research Institute).

———. (1984). "The New Social Security Legislation in the U.S.," *Economia & Lavoro* (18) January/March, pp. 129–134.

Stockman, D.A. (1986). *The Triumph of Politics: How the Reagan Revolution Failed* (New York: Harper & Row).

TIAA-CREF. (1981). *Your TIAA and CREF Annuities and the New TIAA Graded Benefit Method* (New York: Teachers Insurance and Annuity Association).

U.S. President. (1982). *Economic Report of the President* (Washington, DC: U.S. Government Printing Office).

von Furstenberg, G.M., ed. (1979). *Social Security versus Private Saving* (Cambridge, MA: Ballinger Publishing Co.).

3

Intercohort and Intracohort Redistribution under Social Security

Charles W. Meyer
Nancy L. Wolff

For nearly five decades, the Social Security program has grown in scope, worker-coverage, budgetary significance and, until quite recently, popularity. However, the program has entered a new phase marked by public confusion, critical debate, budgetary insolvency and controversy. This essay investigates one cause of the controversy, the income redistribution objective of the program. The old age and survivors insurance (OASI) portion of the Social Security program has two primary objectives: (1) to insure retirees against an uncertain life span in the latter phase of their life cycle when potential earnings are low or zero; and (2) to redistribute income within an age cohort and across generations. The former objective alters the pattern of income receipts across the individual's life cycle, whereas the latter alters the distribution of lifetime income within an age cohort and across generations. Early in its history policymakers began to shift the emphasis of the program away from traditional insurance principles, or "individual equity," toward a distribution of benefits based on the presumptive needs of retired persons and their dependents, or "social adequacy."

The apparent dual nature of the program was not problematic until recently because taxes were kept at acceptable levels, covered retirees were generally net gainers and to a lesser extent, the program was conveniently cast in a traditional insurance-like framework. The first generation of OASI beneficiaries received exorbitant rates of return on prior OASI contributions owing to the fact that they had few years of coverage in the program and a relatively long benefit collection period. Subsequent generations have benefitted from the relative immaturity of the program, which made possible extremely low tax rates and frequent increases in benefit levels. As the system matures, the contribution period eclipses the entire work history, taxes rise, and the size of the intergenerational transfer diminishes. The probability of being a net loser increases, drawing further attention to the cause of the loser-gainer phenomenon — the redistribution objective.[1]

This essay does not address the legitimacy of the redistribution objective; instead, it seeks to examine the program's performance in redistributing income within and across retirement cohorts. Three interrelated issues will be investigated: (1) Does the OASI portion of the Social Security program redistribute income in favor of low-income beneficiaries? (2) Does the current OASI program redistribute benefits in favor of women, as a group, at the expense of their male counterparts? (3) Are spousal benefits a source of discrimination against two-earner married couples? Answers to these questions are needed to assess the effectiveness of the current OASI program in satisfying its intended objectives and to shed light on inequities and inadequacies resulting from specific provisions in the law.

First, we examine the results of several representative studies of intercohort and intracohort redistribution. Included are estimates for both past and future retirement cohorts. Most of the results are in the form of hypothetical examples that illustrate how program parameters affect individuals with assumed characteristics and earnings histories. The remaining results are based at least in part on data from samples of actual beneficiaries.

Next we present results of a study of the distributional impact of the OAI program on a sample of actual beneficiaries who retired during the years 1962–1972. These are the most recent cohorts for which such data are available. The distributional impact is determined by separating the insurance portion of OAI benefits from the redistributive portion. The separation is achieved by calculating the annuity benefit stream that a worker could purchase with accumulated OAI tax contributions and comparing it with actual benefits. The difference gives us a measure of the redistributional component.

The essay concludes with a summary of results and issues relating to distribution of benefits.

Previous Findings

The studies summarized in this section represent a variety of methodologies. Distributional impact is measured in terms of lifetime internal rates of return, lifetime benefit ratios, present value of net benefits (net Social Security wealth), and size of the redistributional transfer component in annual benefit payments.

A number of researchers have investigated the effect of the Social Security program on the distribution of income over the life cycle of workers. Most studies illustrate the effect of the program on representative individuals. A few draw on individual case histories. Thompson (1983) delineates the two conceptual frameworks reflected in these studies. He refers to the first as the insurance model, which compares the expected value of insurance protection with its tax price. This relationship is measured in the form of benefit-contribution ratios, net present values, or internal rates of return. The essential element of Social Security is seen as the pooling among workers of the risk of earnings loss. The second approach, which Thompson calls the annuity-welfare model, decomposes benefits into an annuity component and a transfer or social adequacy component.[2] Most published studies conform to the insurance model.

Chen and Chu (1974) estimated contribution-benefit ratios and internal rates of return for representative workers who retired in 1974 and for workers entering the labor force at ages 18 and 22 in 1974 and retiring at age 65. Their hypothetical examples incorporate program provisions in effect as of 1974. They show lower contribution-benefit ratios and higher rates of return for workers with average taxable earnings than for workers with maximum taxable earnings. As expected, contribution-benefit ratios are much lower for 1974 retirees than for 1974 entrants. Ratios are also lower for 1974 entrants who enter at age 22 rather than 18, assuming equal annual earnings.

Aaron (1977) calculated benefit-cost ratios for representative individuals in a variety of socioeconomic categories. His results are based on earnings profiles derived from the 1967 Survey of Economic Opportunity and adjusted for assumed growth rates in earnings. Results are presented for married and single households arrayed by years of education. Since the benefit formula is progressive and the payroll tax is proportional up to maximum taxable earnings, one would expect, given the positive correlation between education and earnings, that benefit-cost ratios would decline as years of educational attainment rise. Aaron's results show, however, that for white households benefit-cost ratios consistently rise with education. This indicates that the longer life expectancy associated with more education more than offsets the progressivity in the benefit formula. The pattern holds across one- and two-earner married households and for male and female single workers. This unexpected relationship does not generally hold for nonwhites, for whom the pattern is somewhat irregular. Aaron's other findings are consistent with expectations. Benefit-cost ratios are highest for one-earner couples, followed by two-earner couples, single females, and single males. Workers with higher educational attainment gain from other features of the benefit computation formula, which reward late entry and steep lifetime earnings profiles.

Okonkwo (1976) used longitudinal age-earnings profiles from four successive U.S. censuses and life expectancies disaggregated by sex, race, and education to estimate internal rates of return. He found higher rates of return for couples relative to single persons, nonwhites relative to whites, and households in the South relative to the North. He also found that returns vary inversely with education. Okonkwo concludes that OAI redistributes income to nonwhites and low-income whites, but that its progressivity is dampened by differences in survival probabilities.

Freiden, Leimer, and Hoffman (1976) used data from the Continuous Work History Survey to calculate real earning and benefit streams. Benefits streams were calculated for workers only and are based on the primary insurance amount (PIA) as calculated at date of retirement. Survivor probabilities were disaggregated by age, sex, and race. Internal rates of return were calculated for a sample of workers who retired during the years 1967–70. The authors found the OAI program to be very progressive with substantially higher rates of return for workers with low earnings and for women relative to men. For workers who retired at age 65, average real rates of return for men ranged from 23.09 percent in the lowest earnings quartile to 8.56 percent in the highest. For women the corresponding range was from 29.01 percent in the lowest earnings quartile to 9.77 percent in the highest. These high rates of return are indicative of the experience of earlier retirement cohorts.

A simulation by Moffitt (1984) deals only with intercohort redistribution. He estimated net social security wealth (present value of benefits minus taxes) at time of entry into the labor force for eight cohorts. The entry period covered is 1942–77. Wealth rises for successive cohorts, but the growth rate declines continuously. Absolute increments in wealth decline after 1970. Because Moffitt estimates wealth at time of entry, his results account for taxes and survivor's benefits of workers who die before reaching retirement.

Pellechio and Goodfellow (1983) estimated the present value in 1983 of future benefits and past and future tax contributions for a set of representative workers. They developed a computer simulation model that incorporates survival and disability rates, past and projected earnings trajectories, and program parameters. Separate calculations were made for persons aged 25, 40 and 55 at six different earnings levels, ranging from $10,000 to $35,700 (the maximum taxable earnings in 1983). Assumed family situations included married couples in which husband only, wife only, and both spouses work, single males, and single females.

Their results are shown in tables 3–1 (age 25), 3–2 (age 40) and 3–3 (age 55). Their simulation model calculated future benefits by applying the benefit calculation formula to assumed past and future earnings (adjusted for inflation). Intermediate (IIB) interest rate projections in the 1983 Social Security Trustees Report were used to discount future benefits to present values. (These rates ranged from 11.4 percent for 1983 to 6.1 percent after 1995). In addition, benefits entitlements were adjusted to reflect survival and disability probabilities.

Present values of past tax payments were calculated by indexing and adding appropriate interest accumulations. Yearly average interest rates on Social Security Trust Fund special issues were used for this purpose.

Other things equal, net present value (benefits minus taxes) declines with age, is highest for one-earner married couples (especially those in which only the wife works), and lowest for single males. For one-earner couples, net pre-

Table 3–1
Gains and Losses under OASDI for Individuals Age 25 in 1983
(1983 Dollars)[a]

Total Earnings in 1983[b]	Family Situation				
	Husband Works	Wife Works	Both Spouses Work	Unmarried Male	Unmarried Female
$10,000					
SSW	66,383	70,323	55,304	30,483	44,580
PVTAX	40,120	41,724	40,993	40,263	41,724
Gain/Loss	26,120	28,600	14,311	−9,780	2,857
$15,000					
SSW	87,099	92,274	67,863	40,002	58,503
PVTAX	60,395	62,585	61,490	60,395	62,585
Gain/Loss	26,704	29,689	6,373	−20,393	−4,082
$20,000					
SSW	107,446	113,816	80,424	49,041	71,784
PVTAX	80,526	83,447	81,987	80,526	83,447
Gain/Loss	26,920	30,369	−1,562	−31,486	−11,663
$25,000					
SSW	116,909	123,688	92,985	53,023	77,624
PVTAX	100,658	104,309	102,483	100,658	104,309
Gain/Loss	16,251	19,379	−9,498	−47,635	−26,685
$30,000					
SSW	125,936	133,149	105,537	57,000	83,436
PVTAX	120,790	125,171	122,980	120,790	125,171
Gain/Loss	5,147	7,978	−17,443	−63,790	−41,735
$35,700					
SSW	135,434	143,162	119,338	61,271	89,682
PVTAX	141,446	146,602	146,346	141,446	146,602
Gain/Loss	−6,012	−3,440	−27,008	−80,175	−56,920

Source: Pellechio and Goodfellow (1983), p. 437

[a] Some of the gain/loss calculations are off by one unit due to rounding.

[b] SSW = Social Security wealth; PVTAX = present value of payroll taxes; Gain/Loss = net gain or loss.

sent value is highest for middle-income ($20,000 in 1983) couples. For all other family types it is highest for the low earners ($10,000). This illustrates the redistributive nature of the benefit formula. Among the 30 earnings/family-type cells, net present value is negative in five cells (all single males) for persons age 55, negative in 15 cells for persons age 40, and negative in 17 cells for persons age 25.[3]

Ferrara and Lott (1985) calculated rates of return to OASDI for twelve hypothetical family types entering the work force in 1983. Three earnings levels were assumed—minimum wage, average earnings for covered workers, and maximum taxable earnings. Earnings at these levels were assumed to

Table 3–2
Gains and Losses under OASDI for Individuals Age 40 in 1983
(1983 Dollars)[a]

	Family Situation				
Total Earnings in 1983[b]	Husband Works	Wife Works	Both Spouses Work	Unmarried Male	Unmarried Female
$10,000					
SSW	72,447	75,399	57,633	34,685	48,468
PVTAX	43,042	44,094	43,568	43,042	44,094
Gain/Loss	29,405	31,305	14,065	−8,357	4,374
$15,000					
SSW	95,053	98,936	70,730	45,515	63,605
PVTAX	64,563	66,141	65,352	64,563	66,141
Gain/Loss	30,490	32,794	5,378	−19,048	−2,537
$20,000					
SSW	117,515	122,322	83,837	56,274	78,643
PVTAX	85,286	87,391	87,136	85,286	87,391
Gain/Loss	32,229	34,931	−3,299	−29,912	−8,748
$25,000					
SSW	127,601	132,905	96,929	61,157	85,500
PVTAX	102,629	105,260	108,920	102,629	105,260
Gain/Loss	24,972	−27,645	−11,991	−41,472	−19,760
$30,000					
SSW	135,750	141,545	110,016	65,028	91,008
PVTAX	116,830	119,987	130,704	116,830	119,987
Gain/Loss	18,920	21,558	−20,688	−51,802	−28,979
$35,700					
SSW	143,479	149,746	124,943	68,602	96,101
PVTAX	130,430	134,150	155,168	130,430	134,150
Gain/Loss	13,049	15,597	−30,226	−61,828	−38,049

Source: Pellechio and Goodfellow (1983), p. 436

[a] Some of the gain/loss calculations are off by one unit due to rounding.

[b] SSW = Social Security wealth; PVTAX = present value of payroll taxes; Gain/Loss = net gain or loss.

continue from entry at ages 18, 22, and 24, respectively, until retirement at age 67, the normal retirement age for workers of the assumed ages. Retirement, survivors, and disability benefits and payroll tax liabilities were determined in accordance with economic and demographic assumptions from the intermediate IIB projections in the 1983 report of the Social Security Trustees. Assignments of benefits and taxes reflect anticipated probability of death or disability. Low-income, one-earner couples receive a real return of 2.75 percent on tax contributions. Returns for other household configurations range from − 1.5 percent for high-earner single workers to 1.5 percent for low-earner single individuals, two-earner low-income families, and

Table 3–3
Gains and Losses under OASDI for Individuals Age 55 in 1983
(1983 Dollars)[a]

Total Earnings in 1983[b]	Family Situation				
	Husband Works	Wife Works	Both Spouses Work	Unmarried Male	Unmarried Female
$10,000					
SSW	84,971	86,663	67,752	42,067	56,506
PVTAX	37,899	38,339	38,119	37,899	38,339
Gain/Loss	47,072	48,324	29,633	4,168	18,166
$15,000					
SSW	111,518	113,750	83,162	55,218	74,174
PVTAX	56,848	57,509	57,179	56,848	57,509
Gain/Loss	54,669	56,241	25,983	−1,631	16,665
$20,000					
SSW	135,464	138,169	98,572	67,098	90,178
PVTAX	73,034	73,915	76,238	73,034	73,915
Gain/Loss	62,314	64,255	22,334	−5,936	16,263
$25,000					
SSW	143,464	146,455	113,982	71,118	95,584
PVTAX	83,562	84,663	95,298	83,562	84,663
Gain/Loss	59,902	61,793	18,684	−12,444	10,921
$30,000					
SSW	148,249	151,469	129,392	73,580	98,946
PVTAX	90,948	92,269	114,357	90,948	92,269
Gain/Loss	57,300	59,200	15,035	−17,368	6,677
$35,700					
SSW	152,430	155,884	146,894	75,755	101,930
PVTAX	97,264	98,823	134,884	97,264	98,823
Gain/Loss	55,166	57,062	12,010	−21,509	3,107

Source: Pellechio and Goodfellow (1983), p. 438

[a] Some of the gain/loss calculations are off by one unit due to rounding.

[b] SSW = Social Security wealth; PVTAX = present value of payroll taxes; Gain/Loss = net gain or loss.

average-income workers with a nonworking spouse. Family units with high earnings receive zero or negative returns.

Estimates of internal rates of return are important, because they are frequently compared to returns on private investments. Ferrara and Lott, for example, contrast the near zero return young workers can expect from Social Security with the 6.5 percent real return that they consider to be a realistic measure of returns on a portfolio of stocks and bonds.[4] Others have estimated higher real returns from Social Security, even for younger workers. For example, Leimer and Petri (1981) estimated real returns of between 2 and 3 percent for workers born after 1955.[5] Their estimates are derived from a microsimulation model of the U.S. economy. They simulated various responses to the funding crisis, and the choice does affect returns to different cohorts. In no case do their estimated returns to today's young workers drop to the zero range. They make no estimates of intracohort returns.

Among these studies, only Freiden, Leimer, and Hoffman (1976) drew on a sample of actual beneficiaries. All studies cited required projections of future benefits and most required projections of future taxes. None offers a standard of actuarial fairness against which to compare actual benefit payments.

In contrast, the work of Burkhauser and Warlick (1981) represents a new departure. Their work conforms to the annuity-welfare model and draws on a sample of beneficiaries. The data source is a subset of old age and survivors insurance (OASI) beneficiaries aged 65 and over included in the 1973 Exact Match File. Information in this data set allowed them to estimate the accumulated value of each worker's OASI tax contribution at time of retirement. They then calculated the annual annuity payment that the worker could purchase with this amount. The annuity payment depends on the life expectancy of the worker and dependent spouse, if present. By subtracting the annual actuarially fair annuity payment from reported OASI benefits, Burkhauser-Warlick were able to measure the redistributional component in the annual 1972 benefit payment to each household in the sample. Sample households were aggregated by income group with results presented in tabular form. They show that all beneficiaries received payments well in excess of fair annuity benefits. The largest transfers in absolute terms went to middle-income retirees. Transfers as a percentage of total OASI benefits generally declined as income increased, but the pattern was reversed among high-income beneficiaries. Burkhauser and Warlick also found that transfers as a percentage of benefits were higher for earlier cohorts, confirming the results of other investigators.

Taken collectively, these studies provide useful insights into the distribution of Social Security benefits across and within cohorts. The results confirm the belief that returns to contributions were highest for early retirement cohorts, as expected during the start-up phase of a pay-as-you-go retirement system. Results generally confirm the progressive nature of benefit payments within cohorts, but Aaron's contrary results suggest that additional investigation of the effect of differential mortality rates across socioeconomic groups would be desirable. Some of the studies shed light on the relationship between family composition and distribution of benefits. This matter has become increasingly sensitive, given the rise in the number of two-earner families.

Intercohort and Intracohort Redistribution for the 1962–1972 Retirement Cohorts: An Extension of Burkhauser-Warlick

A study by Meyer and Wolff (1986) applies the annuity-welfare model and is similar in approach to Burkhauser and Warlick (1981). An attractive feature of this approach is its focus on individual equity as viewed over the life cycle of a worker. The study sample consists of single persons and retired couples in the 1962–72 retirement cohorts. An actuarial standard of fairness is used to determine how much a retired worker would receive from an actuarially fair retirement program. The transfer component in the old age insurance (OAI) program is then determined by comparing actual benefits paid to a sample of beneficiaries with what they would receive from an annuity purchased at retirement with compounded OAI contributions.

Another feature of the annuity-welfare model is its applicability to policy issues. Some critics of the existing system favor radical reforms that would convert Social Security into a voluntary public system or lead to a phase-out and privatization. In either case the system would assume the characteristics of a private annuity, since in order to be truly voluntary a public system would have to offer coverage comparable to private alternatives.

Although this study employs the Burkhauser-Warlick (BW) methodology and draws on the same data file, it differs in several respects. First, it is limited to OAI. Recipients of survivors insurance were not included because the data file does not contain the earnings history of deceased workers. This information is needed to calculate the annuity. Second, both indexed and nonindexed annuities were calculated for individuals in the sample. Third, a different method was used to calculate the accumulated tax value of contributions. Finally, calculations were limited to the 1962–1972 retirement cohorts.

Study Sample

Data on socioeconomic characteristics, 1972 OAI benefit payments, and claim status for persons in the study sample were drawn from the 1973 Current Population Survey—Administrative Record Exact Match File. The 1973 Exact Match File matches survey records for persons included in the March 1973 Current Population Survey with benefit and earnings information contained in the administrative records of the Social Security Administration and with items from their 1972 IRS individual income tax returns (Kilss and Scheuren, 1978). Longitudinal earnings data for adults in the 1973 Exact

Match File were taken from the Longitudinal Social Security Exact Match File, 1937–76.

Annuity Counterfactual

Observations included in this study are limited to persons age 62 and over who retired between 1962 and 1972 and who received OAI benefits in 1972. A person is considered retired if he or she has filed an OAI benefit claim. Thus some of the persons in the sample continued to work and receive earnings. Only those individuals for whom actuarially fair annuities could be calculated from Match File data were retained. This procedure enabled us to avoid such arbitrary constructs as earnings projections and estimates of future retirement dates. On the other hand, it effectively limited the study to single persons and married couples in which both spouses have filed claims for benefits. Widows drawing benefits on the accounts of deceased spouses were not included because earnings data needed to calculate actuarially fair annuities were not available. Divorced persons drawing on the account of a former spouse were excluded for the same reason. Couples in which only one spouse is drawing benefits were excluded because calculation of the annuity, as described below, is not possible unless the retirement date of both partners is known.[6] The sample includes 353 single persons, 215 female and 138 male, and 1,394 households in the both retired, married set.

The first step in calculating an actuarially fair annuity was to determine the accumulated value of each worker's contributions to OAI at the time of retirement. Because Social Security benefit payments are based on earnings, not on tax contributions, SSA records contain only a history of a worker's earnings in covered employment. A tax algorithm incorporating payroll tax provisions in effect during 1937–1972 was applied to the annual reported earnings of each worker. The algorithm uses the historical OAI tax rate series constructed by Leimer (1976). Leimer used a historical net expenditure decomposition technique to separate past payroll tax contributions into three separate insurance categories, old age (OAI), survivor (SI), and disability (DI). Since this study is limited to OAI, only the portion of taxes attributed that program was included. The accumulated value of each worker's OAI contributions at time of retirement was calculated according to the formula

$$C_i = \sum_{y=B}^{R} T_{yi} \prod_{j=y}^{R} (1 + r_j) \tag{3.1}$$

where T_{yi} = OAI contributions in year y for individual i

r_j = average yield on U.S. government bonds in year j

R = year of retirement
B = first year in covered employment.

The average yield on U.S. government bonds was used to compound the value of contributions because the return on OAI contributions was assumed to be essentially risk-free for these cohorts.[7]

The next step was to calculate the annual annuity benefit that a worker could purchase at time of retirement with accumulated OAI contributions. The actuarially fair annuity serves as a counterfactual against which to compare OAI benefit payments. Separate annuities were calculated for single and married workers. The counterfactuals were designed to mimic the basic features of the OAI system as it existed in 1962–72, the retirement period of the sample population. The counterfactual should therefore replicate an individual annuity that incorporates OAI features while retaining actuarial fairness. It might be thought of as the kind of annuity that would be offered to individuals by the government at time of retirement if OAI were intended to reflect actuarial standards.

The procedure used here enables us to avoid most of the arbitrary assumptions inherent in the other approaches, but two choices remain. These relate to inflation adjustments and choice of a discount rate. During the 1962–72 period post-retirement benefits were not indexed, but Congress regularly legislated benefit increases that equalled or exceeded the rate of increase in prices. This form of de facto indexing continued until 1975 when automatic indexing (introduced in the 1972 Social Security amendments) went into effect. But how does one incorporate this feature into an annuity counterfactual?

Although private annuities ordinarily pay a fixed nominal benefit stream, the annuity formula can be modified to include an ex ante inflation adjustment. The nominal benefit stream will increase at a constant rate that reflects the expected inflation rate over the lifetime of the annuitant. Private annuities do not incorporate the ex post indexing feature of a tax-financed retirement program. Therefore, either a constant nominal (unindexed) benefit stream or ex ante indexing would be a reasonable choice for an annuity counterfactual. The indexed version seems preferable if the intent is to replicate basic features of Social Security.

Both indexed and nonindexed annuities were calculated for individuals in our sample. Estimates of redistribution across income groups using each counterfactual are presented below.

For the calculation of individual annuities we chose a discount rate of 5 percent. This is the rate used by Burkhauser and Warlick, and its use facilitates comparison. They experimented with several discount rates but report that the distributional impact across income groups was not significantly affected. For the indexed annuities we used an expected annual inflation adjustment of 2.75 percent. This is the rate assumed in the Trustees intermediate IIB projection for 1972. It appears to be reasonable for the 1962–72 time period. The discount rate in the indexed annuity formula is converted to real terms. With a 5 percent nominal discount rate and 2.75 percent inflation adjustment, the real discount rate takes a value of 2.189 percent.

Each single worker is assumed to purchase an actuarially fair annuity with the lump sum value of accumulated contributions at retirement. Payments begin at the end of the first month of retirement. Monthly payments depend on the size of the premium, the annuitant's age at retirement, the discount rate, the inflation adjustment, if any, and the survivorship table used in the calculation.

The annuity counterfactual is more complex for married couples. OAI pays a benefit to a retired worker and dependent spouse that is 1.5 times the benefit to a worker only. On the death of either spouse, benefits to the survivor drop by one-third, equalling the amount paid to a single worker. A joint-and-two-thirds annuity duplicates this feature of OAI.[8]

Survivor Probabilities

Two survivor probability tables were used to calculate annuity counterfactuals. Survivor tables give the probability that a person alive at age t, say 65, will survive to age t + 1, say 66. Age-specific (gender merged) tables are based on Social Security survivor probabilities for persons aged 62 and older (Bayo, 1972; Myers and Bayo, 1965). Probabilities for persons younger than 62 are from the Vital Statistics Life Tables (National Center for Health Statistics, 1964). Age-specific (gender-merged) tables do not adjust for differences in survival rates related to sex or other economic and demographic factors. Annuities incorporating a single, age-specific set of survival probabilities thus conform most closely to this feature of OAI. Public debate over Social Security, however, has focused on the impact of the program on disadvantaged groups. For this reason, we have calculated a second set of counterfactuals based on survivor probabilities differentiated by age, race, sex, income, education, and marital status. These tables are from Kitagawa and Hauser (1973) as modified by Leimer (1978).

Behavioral Responses

The actuarially fair annuity was calculated on the assumption of an identical earnings base under OAI or an annuity. Estimates of the redistribution component allow us to examine the effect of various socioeconomic characteristics on the size of transfers and to determine whether the overall effect of the program is consistent with legal intent. The results do not necessarily reflect the effect of a substitution of an actuarially fair retirement system for the OAI program, because no allowance is made for possible effects on factor supply. This is the approach used in the previously cited studies of social security benefits.[9]

Benefit Incidence by Income Group

Average annual OAI benefits and actuarially fair annuity benefits for the sample households are displayed in table 3–4. Households were aggregated into thirteen categories according to total money income in 1972, as reported in the Exact Match File. Money income includes the algebraic sum over all family members fourteen years of age or older. Receipts from sale of assets, tax refunds, gifts, inheritance, and insurance payments are excluded. Where OAI benefits exceeded reported income, income was set equal to the OAI payment. It is clear from the benefit data in column 1 that OAI provided the bulk of money income for households with incomes of less than $5,000. Average benefits per household increased steadily for each group up to $6,000. Above this level average benefits declined slightly in absolute dollars and markedly as a share of total money income.[10]

Actuarially fair indexed and nonindexed annuities were calculated for each household. Annuities were assumed to be purchased with accumulated OAI contributions, as described above. The annuity counterfactuals were calculated using the two survivor tables previously cited. When households are aggregated by income class changes in survival assumptions have almost no effect on average annuity payments. Differences are submerged by the inclusion within each income group of persons of different sex, age, race, educational, and marriage status. Therefore, results are shown for only one set of survival probabilities, those differentiated by age, race, sex, and socioeconomic group. Average annual indexed annuity payments for each income group are shown in column two. Average annual nonindexed annuity payments are shown in column four.

The data in table 3–4 allow separation of OAI benefits into actuarial and redistributive components. The redistribution component for single beneficiaries is calculated as follows:

$$RC_j = \frac{B_{72} - A_n^{72}}{B_{72}} \times 100 \qquad (3.2)$$

where RC_j = percentage of OAI benefits that is redistributive

B_{72} = annual OAI benefits in 1972

A_n^{72} = annual actuarially fair benefit, calculated with survivor probabilities differentiated by age, race, sex, and socioeconomic status.

Table 3–4
Benefit Incidence of the 1972 Old Age Insurance System: Single and Married

Total Family Income in 1972	(1) Mean OAI Benefit Level	(2) Indexed Annuity Counterfactual	(3) $\frac{Col.(1)-Col.(2)}{Col.(1)} \times 100$	(4) Nonindexed Annuity Counterfactual	(5) $\frac{Col.(1)-Col.(4)}{Col.(1)} \times 100$
$0–1,000	$ 698	$ 17	97.6%	$ 19	97.3%
1,001–1,500	1,065	76	92.9	80	92.5
1,501–2,000	1,369	119	91.3	131	90.4
2,001–2,500	1,618	144	91.1	160	90.1
2,501–3,000	1,847	179	90.3	202	89.1
3,001–3,500	2,071	225	89.1	250	87.9
3,501–4,000	2,275	265	88.4	295	87.0
4,001–5,000	2,499	295	88.2	332	86.7
5,001–6,000	2,571	321	87.5	361	86.0
6,001–8,000	2,517	332	86.8	381	84.9
8,001–10,000	2,381	306	87.2	357	85.0
10,001–20,000	2,271	281	87.6	329	85.5
20,001 +	2,425	298	87.7	346	85.7
Mean	$2,283	$274	88.0%	$313	86.3%

For married households the calculation requires comparison of the husband's and wife's 1972 OAI benefits with the annual payments they would receive from joint-and-two-thirds annuities under an actuarially fair program. The redistribution component is calculated as follows:

$$FAM_j = \frac{B_{72} + \bar{B}_{72} - A_n^{72} - \bar{A}_n^{72}}{B_{72} + \bar{B}_{72}} \times 100 \tag{3.3}$$

where FAM_j = redistribution component for family j

B_{72} = wife's annual OAI benefits in 1972

$\bar{B}_{72}$ = husband's annual OAI benefits in 1972

A_n^{72} = wife's actuarially fair benefit in 1972

$\bar{A}_n^{72}$ = husband's actuarially fair benefit in 1972.

The redistribution components as a percentage of monthly benefits, as defined in equations 3.2 and 3.3, are shown in column 3 for the indexed counterfactual and in column 5 for the unindexed counterfactual.

Using the indexed annuity counterfactual we obtain redistributive percentages ranging from a high of 97.6 percent in the lowest income group (less than $1,000) to a low of 86.8 percent for the $6,001–8,000 group. With the nonindexed counterfactual the percentages range from a high of 97.3 percent to a low of 84.9 percent for the same two groups. The redistribution component for the overall sample is 88 percent of annual OAI benefits when calculated with an indexed counterfactual and 86.3 percent when calculated with a nonindexed counterfactual.

This difference is a result of the nature of the payment streams generated by the two annuity formulas. Both annuity streams are purchased for identical sums equal to the value of accumulated payroll tax contributions at retirement. Indexed annuity payments are lower in earlier years and higher in later years than payments under a nonindexed flat annuity. If persons in the early stages of retirement predominate in the sample population, the average annuity payment will be lower and the redistribution higher than under a flat annuity. This is to be expected with a growing retirement population.

For both counterfactuals, these percentages reveal the substantial intercohort transfer paid to persons of this generation who survived beyond retirement age. Estimates of intercohort transfers are somewhat sensitive to the particular parameters used in the calculations, but these results are consistent with other findings of high returns on contributions of persons retiring during this time period.[11]

Evidence of differences in the redistribution component within the sample is also clear. The size of the component declines consistently to a minimum in the $6,001–8,000 income category, then rises slightly in the top three categories. This indicates that the progressive benefit formula does favor low income households within retirement cohorts.

The progressive nature of benefit payments is enhanced by the earnings test, a form of means test that reduces benefits to recipients who continue to work after commencement of benefits. Examination of the households in the data set reveals that only middle and upper income groups are likely to be affected, with the greatest impact among the top four groups. The absence of any impact on the lowest income groups is to be expected, since the first $1,680 of 1972 earnings was disregarded under the earnings test.[12]

Summary and Conclusions

The studies cited above offer convincing evidence of the redistributive nature of Social Security. Large intergenerational transfers are characteristic of the start-up phase of a pay-as-you-go retirement program, and past generations received very high returns from their contributions. Current retirees receive lower returns but enjoy higher real benefits.

Long-term projections indicate that today's younger workers and those who follow are likely to fare less well. If benefits remain at legislated levels, tax increases will probably be necessary. Projections based on a range of economic and demographic trends show returns to contributions ranging from 2 or 3 percent to close to zero. Consequently, program parameters favoring certain groups within each retirement generation will come under close scrutiny.

The redistributive benefit formula favors workers with lower earnings. Shorter life expectancies among the less affluent attenuate redistribution, but most of the evidence indicates that this factor does not reverse the progressivity of the formula. Other features of the program, not reflected in some of the results presented above, also favor the less affluent. Disability insurance incorporates the redistributive benefit formula. In addition, incidence of disability is higher among the disadvantaged. Medicare benefits are independent of contributions once eligibility is established, making this increasingly important part of the system less costly for low-income workers.

The impact of the program on women is less clear. As a group, women gain from greater longevity. Since women's earnings are lower on average, they also gain from the progressive benefit formula. On the other hand, because of dual entitlement many women receive little if any return to their payroll tax contributions. The 1939 Social Security Amendments added dependent's and survivor's benefits. The primary beneficiaries of these features are one-earner families. Indeed, in some cases one-earner families receive higher monthly payments than two-earner families with equal total earnings.

Finally, the system is clearly tilted against the interests of single workers with no dependents. They pay for unneeded survivor's and dependent's benefits. Single males, in particular, fare less well under OAI than other groups because of their less favorable survival rates.

The studies discussed above focus on redistribution within the life-cycle of individuals. An alternative approach is to view the program as a current-period tax-transfer mechanism.[13] Emphasis then turns to the incidence of current-period payroll taxes and benefits. Considerations of tax policy, especially ability-to-pay and horizontal equity, are applied to the tax side. Benefits are judged in terms of value judgments relating to income maintenance, such as concentration of benefits on households with incomes below the poverty level. Judged by these standards, Social Security compares unfavorably with other transfer programs. This is not surprising, because Social Security is a social insurance program, not a welfare program.

The distributional features of the Social Security system are a consequence of a series of decisions made by public officials over many years. Some features with important distributional implications, such as the age-only benefit formula, are accepted without debate. The progressive benefit structure is generally accepted, except for concerns over benefits to uncovered federal employees who attain eligibility from just a few years of coverage. Recent legislation has severely limited this form of "double-dipping." As returns to more affluent workers drop and, perhaps, turn negative, attitudes toward the benefit formula may change. Obviously, any major redistributive features would be incompatible with a voluntary program. Dual entitlement, which favors the one-earner family, appears destined to become a controversial feature. With only about one-third of working families in the one-earner category, political support for the present arrangement might be expected to wane. On the other hand, the pro-family movement can be expected to support the status quo. The debate promises to be lively.[14]

Notes

1. Parsons and Munro predict that the net intergenerational transfer will disappear within 40 years. Workers retiring at that time will have paid high payroll taxes throughout their entire careers. See Parsons and Munro (1977), p. 84.

2. See Thompson (1983), pp. 1436–1438.

3. Pellechio and Goodfellow estimated net present values under pre-1983 and post-1983 legislation. Results reported here incorporate the 1983 Social Security Amendments. As expected, the 1983 amendments reduced net present values for all working-age beneficiaries. Relative net benefits in this study are more reliable than absolute values. The latter are more sensitive to interest rates used in the calculations. Largely because of the somewhat erratic interaction of nominal interest rates and inflation, choice of the proper interest rate is a matter of much disagreement. See Pellechio and Goodfellow (1983) pp. 426–440.

4. See Ferrara and Lott (1985), p. 23.

5. See Leimer and Petri (1981), pp. 20–22.

6. Burkhauser and Warlick (1981) included recipients of survivors as well as old age benefits. They used instrumental variable regressions to assign estimated contributions to deceased workers. They do not report how annuities were calculated for divorced persons or for couples in which only one spouse had claimed benefits. Their study includes all single individuals age 65 and over and all couples in which at least one member is age 65 or over.

7. Contributions are treated like forced savings, impounded until the worker retires. It may be argued that the long-term yield at time of contribution on government bonds maturing in the year of retirement would be more appropriate for compounding than average long-term yields, but such an approach is not easily implemented. First, date of retirement must be known at time of contribution. Second, maximum time to maturity on federal securities is less than time to retirement for contributions in early years, so no market rate is available. The authors devised a bond rollover scheme to deal with the latter problem, but its use resulted in little difference in the compounded value of contributions. See Wolff (1984).

8. The actuarial formulas are described in actuarial texts, e.g., Jordon (1975). The formulas are for an immediate whole life annuity, which pays the first payment one payment interval after the date of purchase and is purchased with a single premium. This is the appropriate form for an analysis of OAI, which pays no benefits prior to retirement.

9. For a summary of empirical results on the effect of social security on factor supply see Aaron (1982), pp. 40–66.

10. To put these income categories in perspective, the consumer price index in 1986 was about 2.4 times its 1972 level.

11. Burkhauser and Warlick (1981) report somewhat smaller transfer percentages, ranging as low as 46 percent of monthly benefits. One reason for the difference would appear to be their decision to include survivors (SI) benefits and, therefore, to include tax contributions to SI in calculating annuities. Since SI benefits are paid to younger survivors as well as to persons of retirement age, the Burkhauser-Warlick calculation includes a cost component not reflected in benefits to persons of retirement age. They also used a higher rate of return to compound contributions. This resulted in a higher present value at retirement and, as a consequence, a larger annuity payment.

12. For an elaboration on the effect of the earnings test see Wolff (1984).

13. Thompson refers to this approach as the tax-transfer model of Social Security. The program is treated as one of several publicly financed transfer programs. See Thompson (1983), p. 1436.

14. For a discussion of the controversy see Lampman and MacDonald (1982).

Bibliography

Aaron, H.J. (1977). "Demographic Effects of Social Security Benefits," in M.S. Feldstein and R.P. Inman, eds., *The Economics of Public Services* (New York: Macmillan), pp. 151–173.

Aaron, H.J. (1982). *Economic Effects of Social Security* (Washington, DC: The Brookings Institution).

Bayo, F. (1972). "Mortality of the Aged," *Transactions of the Society of Actuaries* (24), March, pp. 1–24.

Blinder, A.S., R.H. Gordon and D.E. Wise. (1980). "Reconsidering the Work Disincentive Effects of Social Security," *National Tax Journal* (33), December, pp. 431–442.

———. (1981). "Rhetoric and Reality in Social Security Analysis—A Rejoinder," *National Tax Journal* (34), pp. 473–478.

Burkhauser, R.V. and J. Turner. (1981). "Can Twenty-Five Million Americans Be Wrong? A Response to Blinder, Gordon, and Wise," *National Tax Journal* (34), December, pp. 467–472.

Burkhauser, R.V. and J.L. Warlick. (1981). "Disentangling the Annuity from the Redistributive Aspects of Social Security in the United States," *The Review of Income and Wealth* (27), December, pp. 401–421.

Chen, V.P. and K.W. Chu. (1974). "Tax-Benefit Ratios and Rates of Return under OASI: 1974 Retirees and Entrants," *Journal of Risk and Insurance* (41), June, pp. 189–206.

Ferrara, P.J. and J.R. Lott, Jr. (1985). "Rates of Return Promised by Social Security to Today's Young Workers," in P.J. Ferrara, ed., *Social Security: Prospects for Real Reform* (Washington, DC: Cato Institute), pp. 13–32.

Freiden, A., D. Leimer and R. Hoffman. (1976). "Internal Rates of Return to Retired Worker-Only Beneficiaries under Social Security, 1967–70," in *Studies in Income Distribution,* No. 5, October (Washington, DC: U.S. Department of Health, Education and Welfare).

Jordon, C.W., Jr. (1975). *Society of Actuaries' Textbook on Life Contingencies* (Chicago: The Society of Actuaries).

Kilss, B. and F.J. Scheuren. (1978). "The 1973 CPS-IRS-SSA Exact Match Study," *Social Security Bulletin* (41), October, pp. 14–22.

Kitagawa, E.M. and P.M. Hauser. (1973). Differential Mortality in the United States (Cambridge, MA: Harvard University Press).

Lampman, R.J. and M. Macdonald. (1982). "Concepts Underlying the Current Controversy about Women's Social Security Benefits," in R.V. Burkhauser and K.C. Holden, eds., *A Challenge to Social Security* (New York: Academic Press), pp. 21–39.

Leimer, D.R. (1976). "Identifying Historical OAI, SI and DI Tax Rates under Alternative Program Definition," Social Security Administration. (processed).

Leimer, D.R. (1978). "Projected Rates of Return to Future Social Security Retirees under Alternative Benefit Structures," in *Policy Analysis with Social Security Research Files,* no. 52 (Washington, DC: U.S. Department of Health, Education and Welfare), pp. 235–368.

Leimer, D.R. and P.A. Petri. (1981). "Cohort-Specific Effects of Social Security Policy," *National Tax Journal* (38), March 1981, pp. 8–28.

Meyer, C.W. and N.L. Wolff. (1986). "Intercohort and Intracohort Redistribution Under Old Age Insurance: The 1962–1972 Cohorts," Iowa State University (processed).

Moffitt, R.A. (1982). "Trends in Social Security Wealth," in Marilyn Moon, ed., *Economic Transfers in the United States,* NBER Studies in Income and Wealth, 49 (Chicago: University of Chicago Press).

Myers, R.J. and F. Bayo. (1965). "Mortality of Workers Entitled to Old Age Benefits under OASDI," *Transactions of the Society of Actuaries* (27), pp. 416–431.

National Center for Health Statistics. (1964). *Life Tables for 1959–61* (Washington, DC: U.S. Department of Health, Education and Welfare).

Okonkwo, U. (1976). "Intragenerational Equity under Social Security," International Monetary Fund (processed).

Parsons, D.O. and D.R. Munro. (1977). "Intergenerational Transfers in Social Security," in M.J. Boskin, ed., *The Crisis in Social Security: Problems and Prospects* (San Francisco: Institute for Contemporary Studies), pp. 69–86.

Thompson, L.H. (1983). "The Social Security Reform Debate," *Journal of Economic Literature* (21), December, pp. 1425–1467.

Wolff, N.L. (1984). "The Distributional Impact of the Social Security Program, 1962–1972," Ph.D. dissertation, Iowa State University.

4

Social Security and Private Saving: Theory and Historical Evidence

Selig D. Lesnoy
Dean R. Leimer

During the past decade, debate has focused on whether or not the United States Social Security system has depressed private saving in the economy.[1] In the context of concern about low levels of saving and capital formation and the consequent impact on productivity growth and output, the issue is clearly important.

In a pioneer article, Martin Feldstein (1974)[2] estimated that the introduction of the Social Security system has reduced personal saving in the United States by 50 percent. Subsequent empirical studies by Alicia Munnell (1974), Robert Barro (1978), and Michael Darby (1979) presented estimates variously supporting and contradicting Feldstein's conclusions. Less technical guides to the early debate are provided by Selig Lesnoy and John Hambor (1975) and Louis Esposito (1978).

The debate entered a new phase when, at the 1980 annual meeting of the American Economic Association, Dean Leimer and Selig Lesnoy of the Social Security Administration presented new evidence that cast doubt on Feldstein's conclusion that Social Security had reduced private saving in the United States (Leimer and Lesnoy, 1980, 1982). A second paper reexamining the Barro, Darby, and Munnell studies was presented at the 1981 meeting of the Western Economic Association. The hypothesis that Social Security has reduced personal saving was not supported (Lesnoy and Leimer, 1981). Responding to these studies, Feldstein (1982) presented new evidence supporting his original conclusion. Leimer and Lesnoy (1983) provide an evaluation of Feldstein's new evidence.

This article is a nontechnical presentation of the arguments and evidence, which have previously appeared in the economic literature. After a review of the theoretical arguments, the discussion turns to Feldstein's original empirical evidence, which led him to conclude that Social Security has significantly reduced private saving and how this evidence was flawed by a computer programming error. The core of the article is a discussion of subsequent evidence indicating that currently available historical data do not support the proposition that Social Security reduces private saving. A discussion and critical evaluation of Feldstein's response to this evidence follows, along with a very brief discussion of studies based on international data and household survey data. The final section presents the conclusion that although the total body of evidence—studies based on historical data, international data, and household survey data—is inconclusive, the historical evidence fails to support the hypothesis that Social Security has reduced private saving.

Theoretical Considerations

Arguments for Social Security Reducing Saving

Saving for Retirement. The proposition that Social Security reduces private saving is based on the view that although people save for many reasons—to provide for contingencies, to build up an estate, and to finance children's education, for example—the primary reason for saving is to provide resources for retirement. That is, workers consciously recognize that not only will they be unable or prefer not to work when they are older, but that (in the absence of Social Security system) their consumption during retirement will depend on their own individual resources. During their working years, they therefore build up savings in the form of real assets (such as housing) and financial assets (such as stocks and bonds). These savings are then drawn down toward zero during retirement to finance consumption. This description of household behavior is referred to as the life cycle model of saving.

Aggregate Saving in a Growing Economy. The relationship of aggregate saving to individual saving is not simple. Since active workers save and retired workers dissave (consume more than their income), aggregate saving in the economy depends on the balance between saving and dissaving. In a growing economy, each succeeding generation of workers is generally larger and, because it is richer, saves more than the generations that preceded it. Saving by active workers therefore exceeds dissaving by retired workers, who are both fewer in number and poorer. Thus aggregate saving is positive in a growing economy.

Substitution of Social Security Wealth for Ordinary Wealth. How does the situation change if a Social Security system is introduced into this world in which people save only to finance retirement? Workers contribute during their working years and receive retirement benefits when they stop working. Instead of accumulating retirement wealth in the form of "ordinary wealth"— real and financial assets—workers accumulate retirement wealth in the form of "Social Security wealth"—the accumulated value of rights to future Social Security benefits. This Social Security wealth is measured by the present value of expected benefits less the present value of contributions still to be made.[3] (If the rate of return on contributions happens to equal the rate of return on private saving, the value of Social Security wealth can also be measured by the accumulated value of contributions.) Under this scenario, workers substitute Social Security wealth for ordinary wealth in their portfolios of retirement assets—that is, workers save less for retirement in anticipation of promised future Social Security benefits. This reduction in saving is referred to as the asset substitution effect.

Impact of Pay-As-You-Go Financing. How is aggregate saving affected by Social Security under this scenario? The private saving of each worker is used directly or indirectly to purchase capital assets—for example, stocks and bonds that ultimately finance the purchase of new equipment, buildings, and inventories. Correspondingly, dissaving requires the sale of capital assets. The result for a fully funded Social Security system—one that holds assets equal to the value of Social Security wealth owned by workers participating in the Social Security system—would be similar provided that, directly or indirectly, contributions flow into the private capital market (see digression 1). Contributions would be used to purchase securities. Benefits would be financed by selling securities.

But aside from a small contingency fund, the U.S. Social Security system is financed on a pay-as-you-go basis: contributions do not flow into the capital market; they are used to pay for the cost of current benefits.[4] Thus, if individuals save less for retirement in anticipation of promised future benefits, Social Security will reduce private saving. Total saving will also be less because the Social Security system does not use the contributions to accumulate assets equal in value to promised future benefits. Over time, lower saving results in a lower capital stock, so that aggregate income also will be lower.

Qualifications to Argument

Saving Effect of Inducement to Retire Earlier. The rate at which workers save during their working years depend on their desired level of consumption in retirement and expected age of retirement. The younger the expected retirement age, the higher the planned saving rate—that is, the earlier the worker expects to retire, the longer the anticipated period of retirement to be financed by accumulated savings, and the shorter the available working period in which to accumulate these savings.

Social Security benefits are conditional on retirement. This fact may

Digression 1

Capital Market Effects Require Surpluses in the Unified Budget

If the Social Security system were autonomous, linkage of Social Security funding to the capital markets could be achieved by the purchase and sale of private securities. In actual practice, the U.S. Social Security system can only hold U.S. securities; additionally, Social Security financing is included in the unified budget. (Technically, the 1983 Amendments to the Social Security Act remove Social Security financing from the unified budget effective with fiscal year 1992. From an economic standpoint, the Government will have to continue considering Social Security revenues and expenditures as if they were included in the unified budget.)

A fully funded Social Security system would result in real capital formation only if any surplus in the Social Security fund was associated with a corresponding surplus (or smaller deficit) in the unified budget. This situaton would enable the Treasury to buy outstanding debt. Private sellers of Government debt could then use the proceeds to invest in private capital. Each $1 of U.S. securities held by the Social Security system would correspond to $1 of private real capital. However, if any surplus in the Social Security fund was offset by a corresponding deficit (or smaller surplus) in the general budget, the unified budget would remain unchanged. The Treasury would not redeem outstanding debt and thereby free private sector capital funds. Although the Social Security system would appear funded in the sense that it would hold a large fund of U.S. securities, there would be no additional real capital corresponding to this fund. The net effect on capital formation would not differ substantially from that resulting from pay-as-you-go financing.

---

induce earlier retirement, resulting in a shorter workspan and a longer retirement period. Workers' likely response would be to increase the rate of saving during their working years. In the aggregate, this retirement effect of Social Security would tend to increase the rate of saving and capital formation.[5]

Thus, the asset substitution effect of Social Security tends to reduce the rate of private saving in the economy; the retirement effect of Social Security tends to increase that rate. In principle, depending on the relative strength of these opposing forces, saving may increase, decrease, or be unchanged as a result of the introduction of a Social Security program. For most economists, the conventional wisdom had been that the asset substitution effect probably outweighs the retirement effect, implying that, on balance, retirement saving is reduced by Social Security.

Other Motives for Saving. Most economists agree that the life cycle model has a role in explaining saving behavior. However, increasing concern exists that the role of saving for retirement has been overemphasized and the role of saving to meet contingencies or to leave a bequest has been underemphasized.

The effect of Social Security on saving for contingencies is unclear. On the one hand, Social Security provided retirement income in the form of a joint-and-survivor annuity, and since 1972 benefits have been indexed to the price level.[6] It therefore reduces the worker's need to save in order to protect against the contingencies of the worker or spouse outliving retirement resources or of inflation eroding such resources. On the other hand, unlike ordinary savings, Social Security wealth is totally illiquid and provides no protection against emergencies occurring during the working years. Therefore, it is not clear whether Social Security increases or decreases saving for contingencies.

The effect of Social Security on saving for bequests appears clearer. Social Security wealth cannot be bequeathed. If the worker wants to leave a bequest, he or she must continue saving for this purpose. Indeed, if the worker under Social Security retires at an earlier age, the rate of such saving will be increased somewhat.

The main impact of Social Security—if such an effect exists—is therefore likely to be on saving for retirement. The impact on total saving will then depend both on how Social Security affects retirement saving and on how important retirement saving is relative to saving for contingencies, bequests, and other purposes. For purposes of illustration, suppose that Social Security reduces retirement saving by 40 percent. If retirement saving is 70 percent of total saving, total saving will be reduced by 28 percent; if retirement saving is 30 percent of total saving, total saving will be reduced by 12 percent. Thus, if Social Security does reduce retirement saving, the magnitude of the reduction in total saving is still uncertain.

Limitations of the Life Cycle Model. The life cycle model assumes that individuals have a definite, conscious vision of their economic future—lifetime earnings, interest rates, family composition, and tastes for consumption—and make rational, conscious, and complex decisions in developing and modifying a lifetime plan of spending and saving. Many social scientists are skeptical that individuals are willing or able to make such decisions. The fact that before—and even since—the introduction of the U.S. Social Security program, many workers entered retirement with inadequate resources suggests that workers tend to be shortsighted in the retirement planning decisions or are simply unable to save adequately during their working years. Indeed, this situation was an important reason for the establishment of the U.S. system. Clearly, if in the absence of a Social Security system workers would accumulate only small amounts of ordinary retirement assets, a dollar-for-dollar substitution of Social Security wealth for ordinary wealth could not occur.

Further, some social scientists have hypothesized that Social Security may increase retirement saving. In two separate studies completed in the mid-1960s, it was found that persons covered by pensions saved more than those not covered. One author (Katona, 1965) hypothesized that by making retirement feasible, pension plan participation induced workers to intensify their personal saving efforts to reach their retirement goal. This explanation implies that worker's preferences for spending and saving are not independent of their resources, a view that is inconsistent with the traditional economic model of behavior underlying the life cycle hypothesis. The second author (Cagan, 1965) hypothesized that by participating in a pension plan, workers recognized what their needs would be in retirement and increased their saving; that is, pension plans have a demonstration effect. The life cycle model does not generally incorporate such learning phenomena. To the extent that saving behavior is not explained by the life cycle model, the model cannot be used to predict the effect of Social Security on saving.

Private Voluntary Intergenerational Transfers. To this point, it has been assumed that, in the absence of Social Security, workers would have to finance their retirement out of their own resources. But before the advent of Social Security, many retired workers were supported by their children, who in turn expected to be supported by their children. Thus, the introduction of Social Security may simply substitute a system of mandatory public transfers from young to old for voluntary private transfers from young to old (see digression 2). Alternatively, if, on balance, parents make lifetime transfers to children, they may increase such transfers to compensate for the taxes their children pay to finance the retirement benefits of the older generation. If such transfers are made in the form of financial bequests, workers save less for retirement but more for bequests. Total saving may be unchanged. If such transfers are made in the form of expenditures for education and health, saving for retirement is reduced and spending for education and health is increased. Measured saving will decrease, but in fact there is a change in the composition of capital formation, not its level: more human capital is created — better education and healthier workers — and less ordinary capital — buildings, machines, and inventories.

The foregoing "private voluntary intergenerational transfer model" of Social Security was most fully developed by Robert Barro (1974, 1978). Clearly, to the extent that this model explains the spending, saving, and giving behavior of workers over the life cycle, the effect of Social Security on private saving is reduced.

Ambiguity of Effect of Social Security

To summarize the theoretical arguments concerning the effect of Social Security on private saving:

1. If workers finance retirement out of accumulated savings and if the age at which workers retire is not affected by participation in a Social Security

Digression 2

Rationale for Social Security

The question may be raised "Why have a Social Security system if it simply replaces a private voluntary system with a public system?" One possible rationale is the political judgment that the private voluntary system is too small. In that case, the public system does not simply substitute for the private system. A second rationale is that the public system has an element of insurance not possible in the private system. For the private system, families with few children or suffering unemployment or low earnings may be unable to support retired parents. For the public system, such adverse situations are averaged out. On the other hand, there is the "moral hazard" that workers under Social Security may be induced to work less or have fewer children, which immediately or over time decreases the support available to retired workers.

program, then the introduction of a pay-as-you-go Social Security system will unambiguously reduce aggregate saving. Workers will substitute Social Security wealth for ordinary wealth as they accumulate assets for retirement, while the pay-as-you-go Social Security system will not accumulate assets to offset this reduction in private saving.

2. If workers finance retirement expenditures out of accumulated savings but are induced to retire earlier by Social Security, the asset substitution effect may be offset. By retiring earlier than anticipated, workers will have fewer working years to accumulate savings and more retirement years to dissave, requiring more saving.

3. If workers finance retirement spending out of accumulated savings but also have other motives for saving, such as providing for contingencies or leaving a bequest, then even if saving for retirement is reduced, the effect on total private saving is diluted.

4. If providing for retirement is a major motive for saving, but workers have only vague expectations about the future, or do not make conscious, rational decisions about saving, it is less likely that they will change their saving patterns in response to Social Security, and, if they do, the direction of change may be counter to economic intuition.

5. To the extent that workers finance consumption in retirement out of voluntary transfers from children, not out of accumulated savings, participation in Social Security does not reduce private saving. A similar conclusion is reached if parents increase their bequests to children in order to offset the tax burden imposed on the younger generation by the Social Security system.

All in all, theoretical considerations do not unambiguously predict the effect of Social Security on private saving. It is theoretically possible that Social Security increases, has no effect, or decreases saving for retirement. Even if Social Security reduces such saving, the effect on total saving depends on how important retirement saving is relative to total saving. To measure the existence and size of any effect of Social Security on saving, the empirical evidence must be examined.

Empirical Approach

Historical Pattern

How does one evaluate the hypothesis that the Social Security system has reduced aggregate saving in the United States? One approach is to examine the historical evidence.

A simple—some would say simplistic—approach is to examine the pattern of the private saving ratio over time. Figure 4–1 plots the ratio of personal saving to personal disposable income, averaged over business cycles, for the period 1919–82. (Personal disposable income is income that is available to be consumed or saved.) Over this period, the saving ratio has varied with no discernible trend around an average of about 7 percent. This pattern does not suggest that Social Security has reduced saving.

Although figure 4–1 is suggestive, the possibility remains that the stability of the saving ratio is a historical accident resulting from the offsetting effects of different factors, including Social Security, that influence saving. A more rigorous approach that controls for these various factors is required.

Econometric Modeling

The approach taken by most investigators is to specify and estimate an equation explaining consumption (referred to as a consumption function). This equation includes a variable that measures the influence of Social Security. Theory tells us that consumption depends on permanent income (expected income over the individual's lifetime) and wealth. Further, households hold their wealth in the form of ordinary wealth (real and financial assets) and Social Security wealth. The assumed relationship is:

$$C = \beta_1 Y + \beta_2 W + \beta_3 SSW,$$

where C is consumption expenditures. Y is permanent income, W is ordinary wealth, and SSW is Social Security wealth. β_1, β_2, and β_3 are coefficients (multipliers) of unknown magnitude. They are estimated by using multiple regression analysis to statistically fit the specified equation to samples of data. This article focuses on samples consisting of historical data for the

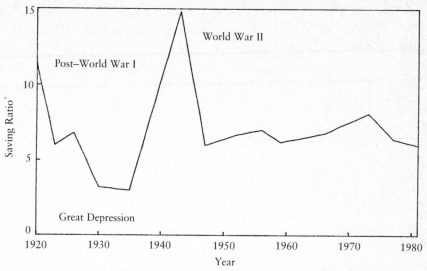

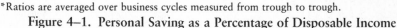

*Ratios are averaged over business cycles measured from trough to trough.

Figure 4–1. Personal Saving as a Percentage of Disposable Income

aggregate U.S. economy. Such data are referred to as aggregate "time-series" data.

Interpreting a Coefficient Estimate

The critical coefficient value is β_3, the coefficient of social security wealth. One important question is "How large is β_3?" For example, assume the average values for the variables are (in billions of dollars): C = \$915, Y = \$1,000, W = \$3,000, and SSW = \$2,000. Suppose the estimated value of β_3 is 0.02. This estimated value implies that for each additional dollar of Social Security wealth, consumption increases by \$0.02. Given the assumed value of SSW consumption is \$40 (0.02 multiplied by \$2,000) billion higher than it would be in the absence of Social Security. Because consumption and saving sum to income, saving is \$40 billion less than it would otherwise be. In this example, Social Security reduces current saving by about one-third: saving with Social Security would be \$85 (\$1,000 minus \$915) billion, while saving without Social Security would be \$125 (\$85 plus \$40) billion.

A second important question is "How sure is one about the estimated size of β_3?" Estimates based on historical samples, like other samples, are imprecise due to sampling variability (see digression 3). The statistical measure

Digression 3

History as a Sample

If a time-series study uses all available historical data, how can the set of data be regarded as a sample? The answer is that the particular set of historical values observed is only one of many potential histories that might have occurred.

The world that generated the observed sequence of consumption values is extremely complex. The major variables used to explain consumption are permanent income, ordinary wealth, and Social Security wealth. A host of unknown variables that influence consumption, including random components of behavior, have been omitted. It is assumed that all of these influencing variables can be represented by a composite variable that influences consumption in a random way.

Consider an "urn of history" containing a large number of balls of different values representing this composite variable. If history draws a ball labeled $+6$, for example, consumption is $6 billion higher than explained by the set of variables; if history draws a ball labeled -33, consumption is $33 billion less than explained by the set of variables; and so on. The sample of recorded historical observations is the result of a particular sequence of actual draws from the urn of history. For the particular history observed, the value of β_3 is estimated and a unique value, say 0.02, is obtained. A different history of draws from the urn can be conceived that would have yielded a different time series of observed values. And for this hypothetical sample, it is possible to imagine estimating the value of β_3, which will likely be a different value. If in this conceptual experiment the balls are replaced each time, this experiment can be repeated over and over, each time obtaining a different estimate of β_3. In principle, then, the estimate of β_3 is a sample estimate, one of many that conceptually might be estimated.

---

of imprecision generally used is the standard error of the estimate. The precision of an estimated coefficient is evaluated by comparing it with its standard error. This comparison can be made in two ways.

One approach is to answer the question "What is the interval that one can be reasonably sure includes the true value?" The conventional interpretation of reasonably sure is 95 percent sure.

The second approach, emphasized in this article, answers the question "What is the probability that the estimated coefficient was obtained by chance if the true coefficient really is zero?" If this probability is less than some critical value, the proposition that the true coefficient is not zero is accepted and the estimate is referred to as statistically significant. If the probability is greater than the critical value, the estimate fails the test and is referred to as statistically insignificant. The critical value is typically set at 5 percent—1 chance in 20.[7] The accepted approach is to place the burden of proof on the hypothesis that Social Security affects consumption (hence savings)—that is, that β_3 is not zero.

For example, suppose the estimate of β_3 is 0.020 and its standard error is 0.016. The first approach is to compute the interval that one is 95 percent sure contains the true coefficient. In this example, that interval ranges from − 0.012 to + 0.052 — a very large interval. Since the estimated standard error is large relative to the estimated value of the coefficient, one is very uncertain about its true value. Alternatively, applying the second approach to this example indicates about 2 chances in 10 of getting a coefficient of 0.02 if the true coefficient is really zero. Since this is much larger than the critical value of 1 chance in 20, the conclusion is that the estimated coefficient is statistically insignificant.

On the other hand, suppose the standard error was 0.008 in this example. The 95-percent-sure interval would then range from 0.004 to 0.036. Although the estimate remains imprecise, the range of uncertainty is reduced. Further, there is now only 1 chance in 100 of getting an estimated coefficient of 0.02 if the true coefficient is zero. The conclusion now would be that the coefficient is statistically significant.

Early Evidence

Initial Evidence

Martin Feldstein presented the initial evidence in an important article in the *Journal of Political Economy* in 1974. To flesh out the specification of the equation, Feldstein measured permanent income (which cannot be directly observed) by current disposable income, the previous year's disposable income, and undistributed corporate profits. But the unique and important contribution of the study was the measurement of Social Security wealth. Two measures of Social Security wealth were constructed: (1) gross Social Security wealth, the estimated actuarial value of future benefits expected by individuals, and (2) net Social Security wealth, defined as gross Social Security wealth less the estimated actuarial value of future payroll taxes that individuals expect to pay.[8]

Although Feldstein presented a number of results, he focused on the equation using the gross Social Security wealth concept with the sample period 1929–71.[9] For this period, the estimated coefficient of Social Security wealth was 0.021, and the estimated standard error was 0.006. Since there is less than 1 chance in 1,000 of obtaining a coefficient this large if the true coefficient is zero, the estimated coefficient is clearly statistically significant. Based on this coefficient, Feldstein estimated that in 1971 Social Security had reduced personal saving by 50 percent.

Confirmation from 1978 Update

In 1978, Feldstein reestimated his specification of the consumption function using revised and improved estimates of national income and its components

(Feldstein, 1978, 1979). The terminal year of the period of estimation was extended from 1971 to 1974 and the initial year was changed from 1929 to 1930. The results were quite close to those Feldstein obtained in his 1974 paper. The estimated coefficient of Social Security wealth was 0.024 and, with a standard error of 0.009, is clearly statistically significant. This result appeared to confirm Feldstein's original conclusion.

Questions about Postwar Results

Results are much weaker when the period of estimation was limited to the postwar period beginning in 1947. In his 1974 study, for the period 1947–71, Feldstein's estimate of the Social Security wealth coefficient was 0.014 with a standard error of 0.030. The probability of obtaining a coefficient this large by chance is about 65 percent, so high that the estimate is considered statistically insignificant. Results for the 1947–74 period were even weaker.[10] The coefficient of Social Security wealth was 0.004 with a standard error of 0.042. The probability of obtaining a coefficient of this size by chance is more than 90 percent. Again, the coefficient is statistically insignificant.

Feldstein has consistently discounted results based on the postwar period. He argues that there is insufficient independent variation in the variables over the postwar period to statistically discriminate among competing hypotheses.[11] This controversial position is examined more carefully below.

Other Time-Series Evidence

Feldstein's article spawned a number of other time-series studies, including those by Alicia Munnell (1974a, b), Robert Barro (1978), and Michael Darby (1979). These studies differed primarily in the specification of the consumption function—that is, in the variables used to explain consumption. The results differed considerably.

Alicia Munnell (1974) used a specification that incorporated the unemployment rate, and, most important, a separate variable to measure the retirement effect of Social Security.[12] The estimated Social Security wealth coefficient implied a negative asset substitution effect of Social Security on saving; the coefficient of the retirement variable implied a positive retirement effect of Social Security on saving. On balance, Social Security was estimated to have a negative effect on saving, but considerably less than estimated by Feldstein.

The consumption function specified by Barro (1978) includes both the unemployment rate and the government surplus (revenues less expenditures) as additional explanatory variables. The estimated coefficient of Social

Security wealth was positive but insignificant for both the postwar years and a longer period that included the prewar years. Barro concluded that although rate time-series evidence could not rule out economically important effects of Social Security on private saving, the evidence did not provide statistical support for the hypothesis that Social Security reduced private saving.

The specification of the consumption function used by Darby (1979) is somewhat different. First, permanent income is estimated as a weighted average of past incomes, with the weights declining exponentially. Second, to explain expenditures on consumer durable goods (automobiles and furniture, for example), Darby includes as explanatory variables the stock of consumer durable goods, the stock of real money balances (the money stock adjusted for changes in the price level), the relative price of durable and nondurable consumer goods, and the interest rate.

For a sample period including both prewar and postwar years, the coefficient of Social Security wealth estimated by Darby was positive but insignificant. For the postwar period, the estimated coefficient was sometimes positive, sometimes negative, but insignificant. Darby concluded that the results may be interpreted as either supporting or denying the hypothesis that Social Security has had an economically important effect on private saving.

New Evidence

In two papers presented in 1980 and 1981, the authors presented new evidence that cast doubt on the conclusions of Feldstein's studies and other studies using the Social Security wealth variable constructed by Feldstein. The first paper (Leimer and Lesnoy, 1980), presented at the 1980 Annual Meeting of the American Economic Association, reexamined the studies by Martin Feldstein.[13] The new evidence had three parts: (1) the demonstration that the original evidence had been flawed by a serious programming error and the construction of the key data series, Social Security wealth; (2) the presentation of empirical estimates using alternative measures of Social Security wealth; and (3) an examination of the sensitivity of results to alternative periods of estimation. The second paper (Lesnoy and Leimer, 1981), delivered at the 1981 Annual Conference of the Western Economic Association, presented a similar reexamination of the studies by Alicia Munnell, Robert Barro, and Michael Darby.

Error in Original Evidence

An attempt by the authors to replicate Feldstein's construction of Social Security wealth revealed that his series was incorrect. Feldstein acknowledged that a computer programming error had been made in incorporating the widows' benefits provisions of the 1956 Amendments to the Social Security Act. As a result of this error, his Social Security wealth series grew too rapidly after 1957. By 1974, the series was 37 percent larger than the correct value.

The estimated coefficient of Social Security wealth is quite different when a correctly programmed replica Feldstein variable is used instead of the incorrect original Feldstein variable.[14] For the period 1930–70, the estimated coefficient is 0.011 with a standard error of 0.011. The probability of obtaining a coefficient this large by chance is about 30 percent. By conventional standards, this coefficient is not significantly different from zero. The result for the postwar period, 1947–74, is more striking. The estimated coefficient of the replica variable is minus 0.060 (implying that Social Security increases saving) with a standard error of 0.020. The probability of obtaining a coefficient this large (in absolute value) by chance is about 3 in 1,000. The negative coefficient is therefore statistically significant. One should not give much weight to the numerical size of this estimate, however. The coefficient implies that, in the absence of Social Security, personal saving would have been $115 billion lower in 1974. Actual personal saving in 1974 was $73 billion. In the absence of Social Security, personal saving under this calculation would have been negative, which is highly unlikely. Nonetheless, this result is clearly inconsistent with the hypothesis that Social Security reduces personal saving.

Unknown Correct Measure

The discovery of a computer programming error in an important economic study attracted much professional and public attention, so much so that the main points of the authors' studies are frequently lost. In particular, the studies demonstrate that the estimated effect of Social Security wealth on personal saving varies depending on the measure of wealth used. This concept is important because the correct measure of Social Security wealth is not known.

Economists generally agree that anticipated retirement benefits represent a form of wealth, but little agreement is found about how to measure such wealth. Unlike ordinary wealth—stocks, bonds, and houses, for example—no objective market value exists for Social Security wealth. A "best guess" of the value that individuals place on Social Security wealth has to be made and that entails making a best guess about how individuals project future benefits and taxes.

Perception of Benefits and Taxes

It is not known how—or even whether— people project future Social Security benefits and taxes. The procedure developed by Martin Feldstein (and followed by the authors with important modifications) for calculating Social

Security wealth assumes that a representative worker acts as if he or she makes two projections. First, the worker projects what the expected income per person will be in some future year. The second projection is what the ratio of average benefits to income—referred to as the benefit-income ratio—will be for that future year. The projected benefit is found by multiplying the expected benefit-income ratio by projected income. The projected Social Security tax for future years is found similarly by projecting the ratio of average tax to income per person—referred to as the tax-income ratio. For example, suppose the representative worker was age 45 in 1975. Real income (income adjusted for changes in the price level) per person in that year was $4,051. Suppose that worker expected real income per person to grow at 2 percent per year. Then real income per person would be expected to reach $6,020 by the time the worker attains age 65. If the anticipated benefit-income ratio was 40 percent, then the projected benefit at age 65 would be 40 percent of $6,020, or $2,408.

The critical question is "Given the observed history of benefit-income ratios, how does the worker project future ratios?" Feldstein assumed that all workers present and past have expected the same benefit-income ratio to prevail for all time. In effect, workers were assumed to ignore changes in current Social Security benefit provisions and changes in the benefit-income ratio during periods between benefit adjustments. Feldstein rationalized this assumption by arguing that workers believed Congress has always intended to amend the benefit formula with some regularity to maintain a fairly constant benefit-income ratio.

The authors view this assumption as overly restrictive. Figure 4–2 depicts the history of benefit-income ratios for beneficiaries currently receiving monthly benefits. The generally declining ratios between benefit formula changes are explained in part by the fact that the benefit formula is progressive and average earnings increase over time. Thus, for a given benefit schedule, as average earnings increase, the ratio of benefits to earnings (income) declines. In addition, benefit levels were not automatically adjusted for inflation until after the 1972 Amendments to the Social Security Act. It seems clear from figure 4–2 that sufficient historic variation has occurred in the benefit-income ratio to raise doubts about an assumption that all workers present and past have expected the same benefit-income ratio to hold for all time. The next sections examine some alternative assumptions.

Alternative Perceptions

No one knows the correct perception of Social Security benefits. The authors' approach was to examine a number of alternatives to see if the results were sensitive to the particular assumption adopted. As examples, consider the following five possibilities.

First, following Feldstein, assume that all individuals present and past

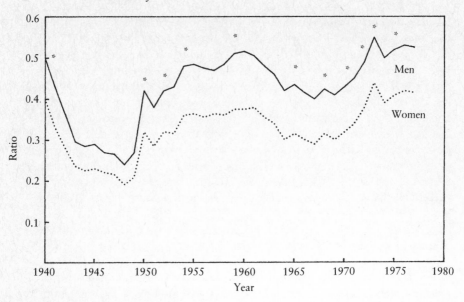

*Years in which benefit formula was changed.

Figure 4–2. Ratio of Benefits per Beneficiary to Disposable Income per Capita

expected the same benefit-income ratio (based on a prediction of the average benefit-income ratio over the period 1940–71). This projection is referred to as the constant ratio or original Feldstein perception.

Second, assume that individuals are shortsighted and simply expect continuation of the current ratio into the future. This projection is referred to as the current ratio perception.

Third, assume that individuals use the most recent observed ratio to modify their previous projection of the benefit-income ratio. This projection is referred to as the adaptive expectations perception.

Fourth, assume that individuals base their projections on the best available published information, namely SSA actuarial studies. This projection is referred to as the best information perpection.

Finally, assume that individuals are prescient and within observed history were able to perfectly forecast the future course of benefit-income ratios. This projection is referred to as the perfect forecast perception. (This perception is considered in part because it parallels the assumption Feldstein makes in projecting tax-income ratios when he computes the Social Security wealth.)

Estimates of the Social Security wealth coefficient based on these alternative perceptions are shown in table 4–1. The period of estimation is 1930–76 (excluding the years around World War II, 1941–46); alternative periods of estimation are considered below.

Table 4–1
Gross Social Security Wealth (SSW) Coefficient and Effect on Saving in 1971: Consumer Expenditure Function Estimated using SSW Variable Based on Feldstein's Replica Algorithm, 1930–76 (excluding 1941–46)

| | SSW coefficient | | | | Estimated effect of SSW on personal saving in 1971 | | | | |
| | Estimated value (1) | Standard error (2) | t-ratio[a] (3) | Probability if true value is zero[b] (percent) (4) | Social security wealth (in 1972 dollars) (5) | SSW effect of personal saving[c] (in 1972 dollars) (6) | Observed personal saving (in 1972 dollars) (7) | Potential personal saving[d] (in 1972 dollars) (8) | Change in personal saving (percent)[e] (9) |
Perception									
Constant ratio	0.005	0.012	0.40	68.9	1,681.2	−8.4	62.9	71.3	−11.8
Current ratio	.000	.005	.02	98.4	2,403.3	0	62.9	62.9	0
Adaptive expectations	.001	.005	.26	79.5	2,300.6	−2.3	62.9	65.2	−3.5
Best information	.001	.004	.20	84.1	2,866.0	−2.9	62.9	65.8	4.4
Perfect forecast	.007	.010	.68	49.7	2,224.6	−15.6	62.9	78.5	−19.9

[a] The t-ratio is the ratio of the estimated coefficient to its standard error. The computed values of the t-ratio are based on unrounded values of estimated coefficients and standard errors. The critical value of the t-ratio for these coefficient estimates is approximately 2 (in absolute value). Column (3) = (1) divided by (2).

[b] This column shows the probability of obtaining by chance a coefficient estimate as large as shown in column (1) if the true value of the coefficient is zero. This probability estimate assumes that the t-distribution can be approximated by the normal distribution for a sample of this size.

[c] Column (6) = negative of (1) multiplied by (5).

[d] Column (8) = (7) minus (6).

[e] Column (9) = (6) divided by (8) multiplied by 100.

All of the estimated coefficients suggest that if Social Security has reduced private saving, the reduction was considerably less than Feldstein estimated. In 1971 (the year Feldstein used to estimate the effect of Social Security on saving), for example, the largest estimated reduction—associated with the perfect forecast perception—was 20 percent; the smallest—associated with the current ratio perception—was zero percent.

More important, the evidence is strong enough for any perception to reject the hypothesis that Social Security has no effect on personal saving. Theory suggests that the true coefficient may be positive or negative. Given this possibility, the chance of obtaining a coefficient of gross Social Security wealth as large as estimated if the true coefficient is zero ranges from 10 in 20 for the perfect forecast perception to 19 in 20 for the current ratio perception. If the theory is interpreted as implying that the true coefficient may be zero or positive, these probabilities should be halved. In no case is the probability value lower than 1 in 20, which is the generally accepted level of statistical significance. It is important to interpret these results carefully. They do not prove that Social Security has had no effect on saving. They do show, however, that the historical evidence does not provide statistically significant support for the hypothesis that personal saving is affected by Social Security.

Alternative Constructions

The second important contribution of the authors' studies was the development of an alternative algorithm—set of rules—for computing Social Security wealth. This algorithm incorporated a number of improved underlying assumptions, the most important of which concerned the probability of an individual receiving retired-worker, dependent-wife, or surviving widow benefits.

Two examples illustrate the differences between the Leimer-Lesnoy and Feldstein algorithms. First, the Feldstein algorithm assumes that a constant proportion of workers of each age will attain insured status and receive a benefit, regardless of the year of computation. In contrast, the Leimer-Lesnoy algorithm projects the probability that an individual will achieve insured status based on projections made by the Office of the Actuary, Social Security Administration. These projections take into account past and projected life histories and changes in the rules for achieving insured status. Second, the Feldstein algorithm assumes that over the entire history and into the future of Social Security, the number of women receiving a dependent-wife benefit is a constant proportion of the number of men receiving retired-worker benefit. The Leimer-Lesnoy algorithm calculates an explicit probability that a married woman will receive a retired-worker benefit. This probability varies by age and year of computation and is again based on actuarial projections of women becoming insured on the basis of their own earnings. In both examples, the Leimer-Lesnoy approach takes into account the substantial changes that have occurred in the labor-force participation patterns of workers and in the rules for achieving insured status. Other differences in assumptions are discussed in Leimer and Lesnoy (1980).

Table 4–2 presents estimates of the Social Security wealth coefficient based on the authors' alternative algorithm for computing Social Security wealth. Three of the estimated coefficients presented are negative, suggesting that if personal saving has been affected by Social Security wealth, it has been increased. The two positive coefficients are extremely small. In 1971, for example, the estimated effect on saving ranges from a 3-percent decrease associated with the adaptive expectations perception to a 21-percent increase associated with the constant ratio and perfect forecast perceptions. However, the evidence in support of the hypothesis that Social Security affects saving in either direction is weak. The probability of obtaining by chance a coefficient as large as estimated if the true coefficient is zero is large for all perceptions, ranging from more than 98 in 100 to about 3 in 10. (Again, the alternative hypothesis underlying these probabilities is that the true coefficient may be either positive or negative.) This evidence clearly does not support the hypothesis that Social Security has an important effect on private saving.

Postwar Evidence Reexamined

The estimated coefficients thus far presented are based on data for the period 1930–76 with the years around World War II, 1941–46, omitted. Because the underlying relationships between economic variables may change over time, economists often estimate results over shorter subperiods to test whether the results differ. If the period of analysis is limited to the postwar years 1947–76, for example, quite different estimates of the effect of Social Security wealth on private saving result. Table 4–3 presents results for Social Security wealth variables constructed using the Feldstein algorithm; table 4–4 presents results for Social Security wealth variables constructed using the Leimer-Lesnoy algorithm.

All of the coefficient estimates are *negative* — that is, the estimated coefficients of Social Security wealth imply that Social Security *increases* private saving. In 1971, for example, the largest estimated increase was associated with the constant ratio perception based on the Feldstein replica algorithm; the smallest estimated increase was 18 percent, associated with the adaptive expectations perception and based on the Leimer-Lesnoy algorithm.

The estimated coefficients for the constant ratio and perfect forecast perceptions are statistically significant whether based on the Feldstein replica or Leimer-Lesnoy algorithm. In table 4–3, for example, the probability of obtaining by chance a coefficient as large as that estimated for the constant ratio Social Security variable — assuming that the true value is zero — is about 5 in

88 • *Social Security*

Table 4–2
Gross Social Security Wealth (SSW) Coefficient and Effect on Saving in 1971: Consumer Expenditure Function Estimated using SSW Variable Based on Leimer-Lesnoy Algorithm, 1930–76 (excluding 1941–46)

| | SSW coefficient | | | | Estimated effect of SSW on personal saving in 1971 | | | | |
| | Estimated value (1) | Standard error (2) | t-ratio[a] (3) | Probability if true value is zero[b] (percent) (4) | Social security wealth (in 1972 dollars) (5) | SSW effect of personal saving[c] (in 1972 dollars) (6) | Observed personal saving (in 1972 dollars) (7) | Potential personal saving[d] (in 1972 dollars) (8) | Change in personal saving (percent)[e] (9) |
Perception									
Constant ratio	−0.006	0.006	−1.01	31.2	1,849.2	+11.1	62.9	51.8	+21.4
Current ratio	−.001	.005	−.14	88.9	2,258.1	+2.3	62.9	60.6	+3.8
Adaptive expectations	.001	.005	.16	87.3	2,125.3	−2.1	62.9	65.0	−3.2
Best information	.000	.004	.02	98.4	2,671.5	0	62.9	62.9	0
Perfect forecast	−.005	.006	−.79	43.0	2,224.0	+11.1	62.9	51.8	+21.4

[a] The t-ratio is the ratio of the estimated coefficient to its standard error. The computed values of the t-ratio are based on unrounded values of estimated coefficients and standard errors. The critical value of the t-ratio for these coefficient estimates is approximately 2 (in absolute value). Column (3) = (1) divided by (2).

[b] This column shows the probability of obtaining by chance a coefficient estimate as large as shown in column (1) if the true value of the coefficient is zero. This probability estimate assumes that the t-distribution can be approximated by the normal distribution for a sample of this size.

[c] Column (6) = negative of (1) multiplied by (5).

[d] Column (8) = (7) minus (6).

[e] Column (9) = (6) divided by (8) multiplied by 100.

Table 4–3
Gross Social Security Wealth (SSW) Coefficient and Effect on Saving in 1971: Consumer Expenditure Function
Estimated using SSW Variable Based on Feldstein's Replica Algorithm, 1947–76

	SSW coefficient			Estimated effect of SSW on personal saving in 1971					
Perception	Estimated value (1)	Standard error (2)	t-ratio[a] (3)	Probability if true value is zero[b] (percent) (4)	Social security wealth (in 1972 dollars) (5)	SSW effect of personal saving[c] (in 1972 dollars) (6)	Observed personal saving (in 1972 dollars) (7)	Potential personal saving[d] (in 1972 dollars) (8)	Change in personal saving (percent)[e] (9)
Constant ratio	−0.068	0.024	−2.83	0.5	1,681.2	+114.3	62.9	−51.4	—
Current ratio	−.006	.006	−.98	32.7	2,403.3	+14.4	62.9	48.5	+29.7
Adaptive expectations	−.005	.006	−.86	39.0	2,300.6	+11.5	62.9	51.4	+22.4
Best information	−.005	.005	−.74	45.9	2,866.0	+14.3	62.9	48.6	+29.4
Perfect forecast	−.042	.019	−2.14	3.2	2,224.6	+93.4	62.9	−30.5	—

[a] The t-ratio is the ratio of the estimated coefficient to its standard error. The computed values of the t-ratio are based on unrounded values of estimated coefficients and standard errors. The critical value of the t-ratio for these coefficient estimates is approximately 2 (in absolute value). Column (3) = (1) divided by (2).
[b] This column shows the probability of obtaining by chance a coefficient estimate as large as shown in column (1) if the true value of the coefficient is zero. This probability estimate assumes that the t-distribution can be approximated by the normal distribution for a sample of this size.
[c] Column (6) = negative of (1) multiplied by (5).
[d] Column (8) = (7) minus (6).
[e] Column (9) = (6) divided by (8) multiplied by 100.

Table 4–4
Gross Social Security Wealth (SSW) Coefficient and Effect on Saving in 1971: Consumer Expenditure Function Estimated using SSW Variable Based on Leimer-Lesnoy Algorithm, 1947–76

| | SSW coefficient | | | | Estimated effect of SSW on personal saving in 1971 | | | | |
Perception	Estimated value (1)	Standard error (2)	t-ratio[a] (3)	Probability if true value is zero[b] (percent) (4)	Social security wealth (in 1972 dollars) (5)	SSW effect of personal saving[c] (in 1972 dollars) (6)	Observed personal saving (in 1972 dollars) (7)	Potential personal saving[d] (in 1972 dollars) (8)	Change in personal saving[e] (percent) (9)
Constant ratio	−0.002	0.008	−2.80	0.5	1,849.2	+40.7	62.9	22.2	+183.3
Current ratio	−.006	.006	−1.02	30.8	2,258.1	+13.5	62.9	49.4	+27.3
Adaptive expectations	−.005	.006	−.79	43.0	2,125.3	+10.6	62.9	52.3	+20.3
Best information	−.004	.005	−.85	39.5	2,671.5	+10.7	62.9	52.2	+20.5
Perfect forecast	−.019	.007	−2.57	1.0	2,224.0	+42.3	62.9	20.6	+205.3

[a] The t-ratio is the ratio of the estimated coefficient to its standard error. The computed values of the t-ratio are based on unrounded values of estimated coefficients and standard errors. The critical value of the t-ratio for these coefficient estimates is approximately 2 (in absolute value). Column (3) = (1) divided by (2).

[b] This column shows the probability of obtaining by chance a coefficient estimate as large as shown in column (1) if the true value of the coefficient is zero. This probability estimate assumes that the t-distribution can be approximated by the normal distribution for a sample of this size.

[c] Column (6) = negative of (1) multiplied by (5).

[d] Column (8) = (7) minus (6).

[e] Column (9) = (6) divided by (8) multiplied by 100.

1,000! Nevertheless, these large negative coefficients should be viewed with considerable skepticism, particularly the constant ratio and perfect forecast coefficients because they imply that personal saving would be negative in the absence of Social Security. The remaining estimated coefficients in tables 4–3 and 4–4 are not statistically significant—the chance of obtaining estimates this large if the true coefficient is zero ranges from about 3 in 10 to about 4 in 10. Clearly, the postwar evidence does not support the hypothesis that Social Security reduces private saving.

Feldstein's Interpretation of Postwar Evidence. Feldstein argues that greater weight should be given to the estimates based on the period that includes the prewar years. His position is based on the interpretation of the estimates obtained for the postwar period in his 1974 and 1978 studies. In the 1974 study, for example, the coefficient of Social Security wealth estimated for the period 1947–71 was 0.014, somewhat smaller than the estimate of 0.021 obtained for the period 1929–71. But this postwar estimate is very imprecise. The standard error is 0.030, more than twice the size of the estimated coefficient. The probability of obtaining an estimate as large as 0.014 by chance is the true coefficient is zero is almost 2 in 3. Alternatively, the interval that would contain the true coefficient with 95-percent confidence would range from − 0.049 to 0.077!

Feldstein argues that this imprecision is due to a statistical problem called mutlicollinearity. A basic problem of analyzing time-series data is that variables frequently move together over time (for example, income, wealth, and a number of other variables explaining consumption all tend to grow over time.) Such movement makes it difficult to estimate the coefficients with precision. In particular, the estimated coefficient of a variable that should have explanatory power, but has relatively little independent movement, may have a large standard error. Feldstein argues that this problem occurs if the sample is restricted to the postwar period. Over this period, less independent variation—that is, variation that is not simply proportional to income—is seen in the Social Security wealth variable. If the prewar years are included, however, more independent variation is observed because Social Security wealth is zero in a number of years before 1937.

Importance of Postwar Evidence. In the authors' view, Feldstein's argument is not persuasive. The imprecision of his estimated coefficient of Social Security wealth for the postwar period is the direct consequence of using the incorrectly programmed Social Security wealth variable. If the replica Feldstein variable is used to estimate the coefficient of Social Security wealth for the period 1947–71, a coefficient of *minus* 0.057 with a standard error of 0.016 is obtained.[15] The probability of obtaining an estimate this large by chance if the true coefficient is zero is less than 1 in 1,000. Indeed, if the coefficient estimates in tables 4–1 and 4–2 are compared with those in tables 4–3 and 4–4, the postwar estimates are more precise (as measured by the t-ratio, the ratio of the coefficient to its standard error) for every perception than the estimates for the full period. The contention that less weight should be given to the postwar period estimates because of their imprecision is not supported by the evidence.

Moreover, the inclusion of Social Security wealth data for the prewar years requires considerable caution. The Social Security Act was passed in 1935. Tax collections began in 1937. When did workers begin to form their perception of Social Security wealth—in 1935 or 1937? Benefits were not scheduled to be paid until 1942, but, as a result of the 1939 Amendments to the Social Security Act, benefit payments began in 1940. The benefit formula differed radically from that passed in 1935. How did workers form their perceptions of future benefits in the period before benefits were first paid? Before the 1939 amendments, did workers base their perceptions on the 1935 Act or were they able to perceive that those provisions would be changed? These questions suggest that the Social Security wealth values computed for the prewar years are especially suspect.

Other Time-Series Studies

As noted earlier, several other studies have been used based on time-series data. Each of these studies uses a different specification of the consumption function—that is, different variables, in addition to Social Security wealth, are included to explain consumption (or saving). To review: Munnell (1974) used different measures of saving and included a variable to explicitly measure the retirement effect of Social Security. Barro (1978) included the unemployment rate and government surplus as well as current and previous year's disposable income and undistributed corporate profits as measures of permanent income. Darby (1979) measured permanent income by a weighted average of past incomes, where the weights declined exponentially. He also included the money stock and consumer durables stock among the variables explaining that part of consumer expenditures represented by consumer durables.

The problem with all of these studies is that they use the incorrectly programmed Social Security wealth variable constructed by Feldstein. Thus the published results are no longer meaningful. The paper presented at the Western Economic Association conference (Lesnoy and Leimer, 1981) contained new evidence based on these alternative specifications of the consumption function but with correct Social Security wealth variables. With some minor exceptions, the authors' conclusions based on the simpler model specified by Feldstein were validated. Although the time-series evidence cannot rule out an economically important effect of Social Security on private saving, the evidence does not provide statistical support for the hypothesis that Social Security reduces private saving.

Debate Continues

Feldstein's New Evidence

In response to the studies refuting his original conclusion, Feldstein presented additional, supporting evidence (Feldstein, 1980, 1982; Arenson, 1980). He contends that the contradictory evidence "ignores the major Social Security legislation that raised the benefits in 1972 by 20 percent and permanently indexed these higher benefits against inflation."

He points out that if the computer programming error is corrected and the period of estimation is limited to 1930–71 — that is, post-1971 data are excluded — the estimated coefficient of Social Security wealth is 0.015 with a standard error of 0.010. Although the estimated coefficient is not statistically significant — the probability of obtaining a coefficient this large by chance is about 11 in 100, which is larger than the critical value of 5 in 100 — he concludes that the result suggests an economically meaningful effect of Social Security on saving.

He further contends that if post-1971 years are included with the 1972 legislative change taken into account (after correcting the programming error), the results are similar to those reported in his earlier studies. The method he uses to reflect the 1972 legislation is simply to increase the corrected Social Security wealth series by 20 percent beginning in 1972. (The resulting Social Security wealth variable is referred to as the revised Feldstein variable.) And indeed, using this revised Social Security wealth variable, Feldstein now estimates that for the period 1930–76 the coefficient of Social Security wealth is 0.018 with a standard error of 0.009. The probability of obtaining a coefficient this large by chance is approximately 5 in 100, about equal to the critical value. The estimate is therefore judged to be statistically significant, supporting the hypothesis that Social Security reduces saving. In addition, Feldstein claims that evidence based on international data and on household survey data also support this hypothesis.

Weakness of New Evidence

How much weight should be given to Feldstein's new evidence? The authors' research suggests the revised estimates provide very weak statistical support for the proposition that Social Security reduces private saving. (Leimer and Lesnoy, 1983, thoroughly examines Feldstein's new evidence).

First, if the consumption function is reestimated using recently revised national income data, Feldstein's results are considerably weaker. For 1930–71, when the revised Feldstein variable is used, the estimated coefficient of Social Security wealth is 0.013 with a standard error of 0.009. The probability of obtaining a coefficient this large by chance is approximately 18 in 100. For 1930–76, when the revised Feldstein variable is used, the estimated coefficient of the Social Security wealth variable is 0.014 with a standard error of 0.009. The probability of obtaining a coefficient this large by chance is about 11 in 100. By conventional standards, neither coefficient is statistically significant. On the other hand, the possibility of a substantial effect of Social Security on private saving cannot be ruled out.

Second, the postwar evidence tells another story. For 1947–71, when the revised Feldstein variable is used, the estimated coefficient is *minus* 0.057 (which implies that Social Security increases private saving) with a standard error of 0.016. The probability of observing a coefficient this large by chance is less than 1 in 1,000. Although technically statistically significant, the size of the estimated coefficient is implausibly large because it implies that private saving would be negative in the absence of Social Security. Nevertheless, the estimate is clearly inconsistent with the proposition that Social Security reduces private saving. For 1947–76, when the revised Feldstein variable is used, the estimated coefficient of Social Security wealth is 0.001 with a standard error of 0.013. Since there are 9 chances in 10 of obtaining a coefficient this large by chance, the estimated coefficient is clearly insignificant. The postwar evidence clearly provides no support for the proposition that Social Security reduces private saving, but it should be recalled that there is disagreement about the interpretation of postwar results.

Third, Feldstein's revised results depend critically on the algorithm used to construct the Social Security wealth series. If the consumption function is reestimated using a revised version of the Leimer-Lesnoy constant ratio Social Security wealth variable—that is, beginning in 1972, the Leimer-Lesnoy constant ratio variable is increased by 20 percent—the results do no support the hypothesis that Social Security reduces private saving. For 1930–76, the estimated coefficient of Social Security wealth is 0.001 with a standard error of 0.007. The probability of obtaining a coefficient this large by chance if the true coefficient is zero is almost 90 in 100. For 1947–76, the estimated coefficient is – 0.009 with a standard error of 0.008. The probability of observing a coefficient this large by chance is almost 30 in 100. Neither coefficient is significantly different from zero. Thus, the procedure suggested by Feldstein to take the 1972 legislation into account provides weak evidence in support of the proposition that Social Security reduces private saving if the Feldstein algorithm is used, but none if the Leimer-Lesnoy algorithm is used.

Finally, the evidence based on alternative perceptions (whether in conjunction with the Feldstein algorithm or the Leimer-Lesnoy algorithm) does not support the hypothesis that Social Security reduces private saving. This highlights a major issue in the debate. Feldstein contends that his revised perception describes individuals' expectations of future benefits better than any of the alternative perceptions that have been suggested. In fact, no one knows how individuals form their expectations of future benefits, and therefore a range of alternative perceptions must be explored.

Influence of Legislation

The most important issue is whether and how both active and retired workers change their expectations of future benefits in response to legislated changes in the benefit formula. As discussed earlier, historically the benefit-income ratio has varied as a result of changes in the Social Security law and changes in economic factors between legislation. How do workers—both active and retired—react to these changes?

Feldstein's view is that before 1972 workers ignored the year-to-year variation in the benefit ratio. They anticipated that the benefit formula would be amended with sufficient regularity to maintain a constant ratio of benefits to income. Beginning in 1972, however, workers perceived a major change in the benefit provisions and immediately adjusted their expectations upward by 20 percent.

The authors reiterate their view that no one knows whether or how individuals form their expectations of future benefits. Indeed, surveys show that individuals do not have precise expectations about the size of future benefits. It is plausible, however, that individuals are aware of legislated benefit increases and recognize that, before the automatic adjustments in the benefit formula, benefits decreased relative to income in the absence of legislation. Since no one knows how individuals form their expectations, a number of alternative perceptions must be considered. Although it is unrealistic to assume that any one of these perceptions captures the diversity of ways in which individuals form their expectations, the conclusions reached in the authors' research are not sensitive to the particular perceptions considered.

All of the alternative perceptions considered by the authors assume that individuals reacted no differently to the 1972 amendments than to other legislated changes. A number of earlier amendments were at least as important as the 1972 amendments. The 1939 amendments totally revised the 1935 benefit formula. Instead of basing benefits on lifetime earnings, benefits were based on average earnings with a lifetime increment based on years of covered earnings. The 1950 legislation dropped the lifetime increment; modification of the benefit formula increased the benefit-income ratio by 30 percent, compared with the average during 1940–49. The 1954 amendments increased the benefit-income ratio by an additional 20 percent, compared with the 1950–53 average. Following the 1958 amendments, the benefit-income ratio rose an additional 5 percent. Despite legislated benefit increases in 1965 and 1967, the benefit-income ratio fell by about 15 percent during the period 1959–69. The combined effect of the 1969 and 1971 amendments was to increase the benefit-income ratio by about 15 percent, compared with 1969. The effect of the 1972 legislation was to increase the benefit-income ratio by an additional 15 percent. And, beginning in 1975, postretirement benefits were indexed to changes in the price level.

The estimated coefficient of Social Security wealth depends on which major legislation is incorporated in the construction of the Social Security wealth variable. Assume, for example, that in addition to the 1972 legislation, both the 1939 and 1950 legislation are incorporated by constructing a Social Security wealth variable with constant ratios for four (instead of two) periods — 1937–39, 1940–49, 1950–71, and 1972–76. If this revised variable is used to estimate the consumer expenditure function for 1930–76, the estimated coefficient of Social Security wealth is 0.005 with a standard error of 0.008. The probability of obtaining a coefficient this large by chance is more than 50 in 100. For 1947–76, the estimated coefficient is -0.012 with a standard error of 0.012. The probability of obtaining a coefficient this large by chance is about 30 in 100. Neither coefficient is statistically significant. Thus, if the revised Feldstein variable is revised further to incorporate the 1939 and 1950 amendments, the evidence supports neither the proposition that Social Security reduces saving nor the proposition that it increases saving.

Further, Feldstein is incorrect in stating that the 1972 legislation was ignored in the authors' research. It is true that the constant ratio perception (also referred to as the original Feldstein perception) does not reflect the 1972 amendments. This perception was considered, however, both because it was necessary to adopt Feldstein's original perceptions in replicating his 1974 and 1978 studies and because the constant ratio perception was considered to be of conceptual interest.[16]

All the alternative perceptions used in the authors' research, however, reflect the 1972 legislated increase. Indeed, it should be clear from the earlier discussion that the authors' research was motivated by skepticism that the constant ratio perception was consistent with the historic variation in the benefit-income ratio associated with changes in the Social Security law and declines in the benefit-income ratio between legislation. It was important to test alternative assumptions about how individuals' perceptions were affected by such changes. This approach differs from Feldstein's in that these alternative perceptions also reflect all other legislated changes in the benefit formula.

Summarizing Time-Series Evidence

The time-series evidence may be summarized as follows: the positive and significant estimate of the revised Social Security wealth coefficient obtained by Feldstein does somewhat increase the uncertainty about the effect of Social Security wealth. Certainly it is possible that he is right and that Social Security has depressed private saving. But, in addition to variants of Feldstein's revised variable, the authors have estimated the coefficient of gross and net Social Security wealth over two periods—a longer period including both prewar and postwar years, and a shorter period limited to the postwar period—using Social Security wealth variables based on 10 reasonable perceptions in the context of two alternative sets of assumptions for constructing Social Security wealth. Some coefficients were positive (implying a reduction in saving) but insignificant; some were negative (implying an increase in saving) and insignificant; a few were negative and significant but implausibly large. The weight of the time-series evidence does not provide statistical support for the proposition that Social Security has reduced personal saving in the United States.

Other Evidence

Feldstein contends that analyses of other types of data—crosscountry and household—support his conclusion. These other studies are considered briefly below.

International Studies in Conflict. A number of studies have used samples consisting of observations of saving/income ratios for industrialized countries. Two studies by Feldstein (1977, 1980a) conclude that Social Security reduces saving. A study by Barro and MacDonald (1979) concludes that the estimated effect differs depending on how the equation is specified. Kopits and Gotur (1980) conclude that saving is positively related to Social Security retirement programs but negatively related to other Social Security programs. Koskela and Viren (1983) find that the Social Security variables used in their study have no effect on household saving. Modigliani and Sterling (1983) find it difficult to obtain a relaible estimate of the effect of Social Security on saving. Clearly no consensus emerges based on this evidence concerning the effect of Social Security on private saving.

Mixed Conclusions of Household Surveys. The other major body of evidence consists of studies using surveys of individual households. Again, this evidence is quite mixed. Feldstein (1983), Feldstein and Pellechio (1979), and

Diamond and Hausman (1984) conclude that the evidence supports the hypothesis that Social Security wealth substitutes for accumulation of private assets. Friedman (1982), Kotlikoff (1979), and Kurz (1981) conclude that the evidence does not support the hypothesis that Social Security wealth substitutes for private wealth accumulation. Blinder, Gordon, and Wise (1983) find that although their model suggests some displacement of private savings by Social Security, the estimated effect is too imprecise and too unstable to draw any conclusions. These divergent results simply compound the uncertainty surrounding the effect of Social Security on private saving.

Conclusion

At first glance, the argument that Social Security reduces private saving appears quite plausible. But as one delves into the complexity of the saving process—the effect of induced earlier retirement, other motives for saving such as emergencies and bequests, shortsighted planning, demonstration effects, and voluntary transfers between generations—it becomes equally plausible that Social Security may have little or no effect on private saving, and indeed it may even increase saving.

The authors' assessment is that if all available empirical evidence—time-series, international comparisons, and household surveys—is considered the evidence is inconclusive. If only time-series data are considered, the evidence fails to support the hypothesis that Social Security has reduced saving. Again, it is important to interpret these results carefully. These results do not prove that Social Security has had no effect on private saving. They do show, however, that the time-series data provide little support for the claim that Social Security has significantly depressed saving in the United States.

Notes

1. This debate is concerned only with the effect of old age retirement and survivor benefits on private saving.

2. Source documents cited in text refer to author and year of publication. The full citations are grouped under references at the end of this article.

3. The present value of a series of payments to be received in the future is that amount which if placed in an interest-bearing account today would just permit withdrawal of the future series of payments, and would be drawn to zero after the final payment. For example, the present value, at 4 percent interest per year, of a series of 10 payments of $100 per year, to be paid at the end of each year, is $811.09. This amount, if placed in an account paying 4 percent interest per year, would permit withdrawal of $100 at the end of each year.

4. Since the Social Security system has not accumulated assets equal to the liability of promised future benefits, the Social Security wealth that individuals hold represents a claim against the earnings of future generations rather than a claim against existing real assets. No real capital corresponds to Social Security wealth.

5. The effect on aggregate saving of an earlier retirement age is complex. Suppose, for example, that the retirement age is reduced from age 70 to 65. Active workers will save more until retirement. But from age 65 to 70, they will be dissaving during a period in which formula they would have been saving. The effect on aggregate saving depends on the balance of additional saving by workers versus dissaving by retirees. It is generally assumed that aggregate saving will increase if the retirement age is reduced.

6. After retirement, the benefit amount is adjusted each year for the increase in the Consumer Price Index (CPI). For example, if the CPI has increased by 4 percent in the past year, the benefit is increased by 4 percent.

7. In practice, the ratio of the coefficient estimate to its standard error—referred to as the sample "t-ratio" or "t-statistic"—is computed and compared to its critical value. If the critical probability value is set at 5 percent, the critical value of the t-ratio is approximately 2 for reasonably large samples.

8. A detailed discussion of the construction of these variables can be found in Leimer and Lesnoy (1980).

9. The years around World War II, 1941–46, are excluded. The postwar period begins with 1947.

10. Postwar coefficients were estimated by the authors. Feldstein did not publish postwar results in his 1978 study.

11. See Feldstein (1979) p. 39.

12. Unlike other authors, Munnell used saving as the variable to be explained. The saving variable was derived from national wealth accounts. The consumer expenditures variable used by other authors was based on the National Income and Product Accounts.

13. Leimer and Lesnoy (1982) present a shortened published version of this paper.

14. Since the authors' original presentation, Feldstein has corrected and revised his variable. To minimize confusion, his original incorrect variable will be referred to as the original Feldstein variable, the same variable with the programming error corrected will be referred to as the corrected Feldstein variable, and his variable with the programming error corrected and with revised assumptions will be referred to as the revised Feldstein variable. The variable called the replica Feldstein variable is the authors' version of the corrected Feldstein variable and yields essentially identical results. To facilitate comparisons with the authors' other estimates, the replica variable is used.

15. A similar result is obtained if the corrected Feldstein variable is used (see note 13).

16. Feldstein, in 1974 and again in 1978 and 1979, used the constant ratio perception. The revised perception was developed after the computer programming error was brought to Feldstein's attention (Arenson, 1980).

Bibliography

Aaron, H.J. (1982). *Economic Effects of Social Security* (Washington, DC. The Brookings Institution).

Arenson, K.W. (1980). "Martin Feldstein's Computer Error," *New York Times,* October 5.

Barro, R.J. (1974). "Are Government Bonds Net Wealth?" *Journal of Political Economy* (82), November/December, pp. 1095–1117.

———. (1978). *The Impact of Social Security on Private Saving* (Washington, DC: American Enterprise Institute).

——— and G.M. Macdonald. (1979). "Social Security and Consumer Spending in an International Cross Section," *Journal of Public Economics* (11), June, pp. 275–289.

Blinder, A.S., R. Gordon and D.E. Wise. (1983). "Social Security, Bequests, and the Life Cycle Theory of Saving: Cross-sectional Tests," in F. Modigliani and R.E. Hemming, eds., *The Determinants of National Saving and Wealth* (London: Macmillan), pp. 89–122.

Cagan, P. (1965). *The Effect of Pension Plans on Aggregate Saving* (New York: National Bureau of Economic Research).

Danziger, S., R. Haveman, and R. Plotnick. (1981). "How Income Transfer Affect Work, Savings, and the Income Distribution: A Critical Review," *Journal of Economic Literature* (19), September, pp. 975–1028.

Darby, M.R. (1979). *The Effects of Social Security on Income and the Capital Stock* (Washington, DC: American Enterprise Institute).

Diamond, P.A. and J.A. Hausman. (1984). "Individual Retirement and Savings Behavior," *Journal of Public Economics* (23), February/March 1984, pp. 81–114.

Esposito, L. (1978). "Effect of Social Security on Private Saving: Review of Studies Using U.S. Time-Series Data," *Social Security Bulletin* (37), May, pp. 9–17.

Feldstein, M.S. (1974). "Social Security, Induced Retirement, and Aggregate Capital Formation," *Journal of Political Economy* (82), September/October, pp. 905–926.

———. (1977). "Social Security and Private Saving: International Evidence in an Extended Life Cycle Model," in M.S. Feldstein and R. Inman, eds., *The Economics of Public Services* (New York: Macmillan).

———. (1978). "Reply," in R.J. Barro, *The Impact of Social Security on Private Saving* (Washington, DC: American Enterprise Institute), pp. 37–47.

———. (1979). in "Social Security and Private Saving: Another Look," comments by R.J. Barro, M.R. Darby, M.S. Feldstein, and A.H. Munnell, *Social Security Bulletin* (42), May, pp. 36–39.

———. (1980a). "International Differences in Social Security and Savings." *Journal of Public Economics* (14), October, pp. 225–244.

———. (1980b). "Social Security, Induced Retirement and Aggregate Capital Accumulation: A Correction and Updating," National Bureau of Economic Research Working Paper No. 579.

———. (1982). "Social Security and Private Saving: Reply," *Journal of Political Economy* (90), June, pp. 630–642.

————. (1983). "Social Security Benefits and the Accumulation of Preretirement Wealth," in F. Modigliani and R.E. Hemming, eds., (London: Macmillan), pp. 3–23.

———— and Anthony Pellechio. (1979). "Social Security and Household Wealth Accumulation: New Microeconomic Evidence," *Review of Economics and Statistics* (61), August, pp. 361–368.

Friedman, J. (1982). "Asset Accumulation and Depletion Among the Elderly," paper prepared for the Brookings Institution Conference on Retirement and Aging, October 21–22.

Katona, G. (1965). *Private Pensions and Individual Saving* (Ann Arbor: Institute for Social Research, University of Michigan).

Kopits, G. and P. Gotur. (1980). "The Influence of Social Security on Household Saving: A Cross-Country Investigation," *Intergenerational Monetary Fund Staff Papers* (27), March, pp. 161–190.

Koskela, E. and M. Viren. (1983). "Social Security and Household Saving in an International Cross Section," *American Economic Review* (73), pp. 212–217.

Kotlikoff, L.J. (1979). "Testing the Theory of Social Security and Life Cycle Accumulation," *American Economic Review* (69), June, pp. 396–410.

Kurz, M. (1981). "The Life Cycle Hypothesis and the Effects of Social Security and Private Pensions on Family Saving," Institute for Mathematical Studies in the Social Sciences, Stanford University.

Leimer, D.R. and S.D. Lesnoy. (1980). "Social Security and Private Saving: A Reexamination of the Time-Series Evidence Using Alternative Social Security Wealth Variables," Office of Research and Statistics, Social Security Administration, Working Paper No. 19.

———— and ————. (1982). "Social Security and Private Saving: New Time-Series Evidence," *Journal of Political Economy* (90), June, pp. 606–629.

———— and ————. (1983). "Social Security and Private Saving: An Examination of Feldstein's New Evidence," Office of Research, Statistics, and International Policy, Social Security Administration, Working Paper No. 31.

Lesnoy, S.D. and J.C. Hambor. (1975). "Social Security, Saving, and Capital Formation," *Social Security Bulletin* (38), July, pp. 3–15.

———— and D.R. Leimer. (1981). "Social Security and Private Saving: New Time-Series Evidence with Alternative Specifications," Office of Research and Statistics, Social Security Administration, Working Paper No. 22.

Modigliani, F. and A. Sterling. (1983). "Determinants of Private Saving with Special Reference to the Role of Social Security—Cross-Country Tests," in F. Modigliani and R. Hemming, eds., *The Determinants of National Saving and Wealth* (London: Macmillan) pp. 24–55.

Munnell, A.H. (1974a). *The Effect of Social Security on Personal Saving* (Cambridge, MA: Ballinger Publishing Co.).

————. (1974b). "The Impact of Social Security on Personal Saving," *National Tax Journal,* April, pp. 553–568.

5

Labor Market Behavior of Older Workers Approaching Retirement: A Summary of the Evidence from the 1970s

Rachel Floersheim Boaz

The Social Security system, which was inaugurated by President Franklin D. Roosevelt as a response to the massive unemployment of the Great Depression, initiated the public policy that workers who reach age 65 would be entitled to a public pension for their remaining lifetime. Thus, age 65 has become the accepted age of retirement from paid work in the United States. In 1967, Congress affirmed this acceptance when it passed the Age Discrimination in Employment Act (ADEA), outlawing age-based discrimination in employment until age 65. In 1978, when Congress amended ADEA and extended protection against this discrimination to age 70, it continued to hold onto the perception that age 65 was not an early age of retirement and permitted employers to stop pension-accruals beyond age 65. However, during the past two decades, many men have ceased working at their primary career jobs and have dropped out of the labor-force before they reached that age, and this development has been reflected in the increased number of early recipients (before age 65) of Social Security retired-worker benefits.

The trend toward early withdrawal from the labor market for reasons other than impaired health has triggered an intense public debate about the economic incentives generated by the Social Security system, especially by the availability of retired-worker benefits before age 65. The policy-relevant issue is whether such permanently reduced annual benefits have inadvertently encouraged workers to curtail their labor supply and retire earlier than they otherwise would; or whether, as Congress initially intended, these reduced annual benefits have accommodated individual workers who have lost earnings for reasons which are not related to the rules of the Social Security system. This review focuses on the role of the Social Security provisions which affect earnings and benefits as distinct from the effects of other economic

The author would like to thank Charlotte Muller and Bruno Stein for their comments and Franco Pignataro for his word processing.

incentives on the labor market behavior of older workers approaching retirement. Section I outlines the major developments which are contemporaneous with the trend toward early exit from the labor market. Section II reviews the evidence on the labor supply response to Social Security benefits and employer-provided pensions. Section III discusses the evidence on employers' personnel policies and practice which might induce early retirement. A concluding section assesses the implications of the evidence for public policy.

Major Developments Which are Contemporaneous with the Trend toward Early Retirement

It is expected that labor force participation decreases at older ages. Table 5–1 shows that labor force participation rates decline for all men over age 34 and that this decline is more pronounced for men over age 54 than for younger men. Women's steady influx into the labor market since 1950 has delayed the decrease in their age-specific participation rates until age 65. But when women's participation rates at older ages are compared with their own participation rate at ages 35 to 44, the trend over time does not differ very much from the comparable trend for men.

The rapid decline in the labor force participation of middle-age men has been unexpected. Since 1960, this trend has been contemporaneous with four other developments that may be related to the early exit from the labor market: (1) the improved Social Security disability insurance (DI) benefits during the 1960s and 1970s, (2) the younger age of entitlement to Social Security old age insurance (OAI) benefits since 1961, (3) the rapid expansion of employer-provided pensions since 1950 and the proliferation of early pension options during the 1960s and 1970s, and (4) the influx of large size (baby boom) cohorts into the labor market during the 1960s and 1970s. Each of these developments is briefly described hereafter.

The increase in the real value of DI benefits and in the number of awards occurred during the same time period as the decline in the labor force participation of middle-aged men.[1] Chirikos and Nestel (1981) find that the functional health impairments which are interfering with work have frequently led to exit from the labor market rather than to job reassignments. Parsons (1980, 1982) determines that men whose earnings-capacity is low (low level of education) are more willing than men with higher earnings-power to stop working for the duration (five or six months) of the waiting period required to qualify for DI benefits. He concludes that the availability of DI benefits and their increased amount relative to earnings have been the major cause of the decline in male labor-force participation during the 1960s and 1970s. This conclusion suggests that a tightening of the eligibility requirements would not only reduce the outlay of the DI program but would also reverse

Table 5–1
Labor Force Participation Rates by Age

Age	1960	1965	1970	1975	1980	1985
			Men			
35–44	99.7	97.3	96.9	95.7	95.5	95.0
45–54	95.7	95.6	94.2	92.1	91.2	91.0
55–64	86.8	84.6	83.0	75.8	72.3	67.9
≥ 65	33.1	27.9	26.8	21.7	19.1	15.8
Ratio to 35–44						
45–54	.960	.983	.972	.962	.955	.958
55–64	.871	.869	.857	.792	.757	.715
≥ 65	.332	.287	.277	.227	.200	.166
			Women			
35–44	43.4	46.1	51.1	55.8	65.5	71.8
45–54	49.8	50.9	54.4	54.6	55.9	64.4
55–64	37.2	41.1	43.0	41.0	41.5	42.0
≥ 65	10.8	10.0	9.7	8.3	8.1	7.3
Ratio to 35–44						
45–54	1.147	1.104	1.065	.978	.853	.897
55–64	.857	.892	.841	.735	.633	.585
≥ 65	.249	.217	.174	.149	.124	.102

Source: Bureau of Labor Statistics: *Handbook of Labor Statistics* and *Employment and Earnings*, annual data (e.g., 1985: January 1986, p. 154).

the decline in labor force participation of middle-aged men. This chapter does not consider the effect of DI benefits on the labor market behavior because it focuses on workers' response to economic incentives which are *not* conditioned on health status.

Historically, the Social Security system has viewed age 65 as the acceptable age of retirement at which the full amount of old age insurance (OAI) benefits is awarded. But, since 1961, all workers who have met the vesting requirements for benefit-entitlement can apply for permanently reduced annual benefits at age 62.[2] Quarterly tables in the *Social Security Bulletin* (e.g., table Q–2 in March 1986) show that the proportion of beneficiaries receiving permanently reduced annual benefits has been increasing steadily over time and that it is higher for women than for men. At the end of 1985, 61 percent of all male beneficiaries and 71 percent of all female beneficiaries were receiving such permanently reduced benefits.

In 1961, when the age of entitlement to OAI benefits was reduced from 65 to 62, it was expected that only a minority of men would avail themselves of permanently reduced annual benefits; it was assumed that only workers who had suffered an irreversible earnings-loss would file for benefits before age 65. Hence, the fact that the majority of beneficiaries are receiving permanently reduced benefits has come as a surprise. It has led to a public debate over the question whether the rules governing the availability of Social Security benefits have encouraged workers to apply for early benefits and to walk away from their career jobs earlier than they otherwise would. An affirmative answer to this question implies that the Social Security rules which affect the timing of benefit-acceptance should be changed in order to encourage potential beneficiaries to continue work and delay retirement. The debate over the effect of Social Security rules on the labor market behavior of older workers is the focus of this review and is discussed in subsequent sections.

Employer-provided pensions (PP) provide retirement income to a selected group of employees. Pension coverage expanded rapidly during the 1950s, 1960s and the early 1970s. However, pension coverage does not necessarily entitle workers to pension income because entitlement is based on meeting vesting requirements. Prior to 1974, each employer could determine vesting rights at will. But after many reported abuses, which deprived even long-tenured employees of their pension income, Congress passed the 1974 Employees Retirement Income Security Act (ERISA) which specified the conditions for vested pension rights. As a result, the proportion of full-time covered employees who are vested in an employer-provided pension upon retirement has increased after 1974 (Rogers, 1981, table 3). Hence, although only a selected group of employees has employer-provided pensions when they retire, the role of such pensions in affecting the retirement decision of older workers is likely to have been enhanced since 1974.

Moreover, since the mid-1960s, an increasing number of pension plans, in both the public and the private sectors, revised their rules so that senior employees could qualify for pensions before the age of mandatory retirement.[3] The Federal government and many state and local governments have permitted (and sometimes even encouraged) the early retirement of civilian employees in nonhazardous professions.[4] Also, an increasing number of pension plans in the private sector have been offering early pensions at age 55 or at any age if employees have completed 30 years of service (Meier and Dittmar, 1980, pp. 20–22). In defined-benefit plans, employers can vary the pension amounts not only by the duration of company-service and level of earnings, but also by the age at which the pension is accepted. Hence, employers have been using the early pension option in periods of retrenchment to effect the departure of employees with considerable seniority.[5] Such a personnel policy has been designed to lessen the impact of involuntary termination on younger employees with fewer seniority rights.

Today's young workers with low seniority are members of the baby-boom generation, born between 1946 and 1960. The entry into the labor market of successive large birth-cohorts has had a cumulative effect since the

Table 5–2
Age Composition of the Civilian Labor Force, 1960–1980
(percent)

Age	1960	1965	1970	1975	1980
16–34	37.2	38.1	42.2	48.1	50.4
35–44	23.4	22.6	19.9	18.1	19.3
45–54	21.3	21.2	20.5	18.5	16.2
≥55	18.1	18.1	17.5	15.3	14.1
Total	100.0	100.0	100.0	100.0	100.0

Source: Russell (1982), p. 52.

mid-1960s. Freeman (1979) shows that the earnings differential between men age 45 to 54 and all younger men increased substantially between 1968 and 1977; he concludes that the increased size of the baby-boom cohorts relative to cohorts born in the 1920s and 1930s depressed the earnings of the younger cohorts whereas the earnings of the older cohorts were almost unaffected. Table 5–2 shows the extent to which the age composition of the labor force changed between 1960 and 1980. In 1960, 37 percent of all labor force participants were under age 35; but the relative share of this age group increased over time so that it reached the mark of half the labor force in 1980. Given the large supply of younger workers at relatively lower earnings, employers may have found it advantageous to replace their older employees with younger workers.

It remains to be seen how these contemporaneous developments relate to the early withdrawal of older male workers from the labor force. However, this review is limited to examining the evidence on the extent to which the decision to retire is a response to the availability of earnings-replacing income such as OAI benefits and employer-provided pensions (PP), and the extent to which the retirement decision is a reaction against labor market conditions which evolve from employers' economic disincentives to retain and hire older workers.

The Timing of Retirement as a Labor-Supply Response to Social Security Rules

Age-related retirement is characterized by a considerable reduction in the amount of time which an older worker allocates to paid work; at the limit, retirement is a complete and irreversible withdrawal from the labor market because of old age. The amount of time devoted to market (paid) work may change gradually or abruptly; but ultimately, there comes a time in each person's life when market work is no longer possible because of the frailty that is associated with old age. Yet, the timing of retirement is often unrelated to health problems. Economic incentives which are not conditioned on health status may be a major cause of early retirement. This section examines the role of Social Security rules against the role of employer-provided pensions in affecting the labor supply of older workers and determining the age at which older workers retire.

The economic analysis of labor supply by older workers approaching retirement is based on the theory of how individuals allocate their time between market (paid) work and nonmarket activity or leisure. It is assumed that each individual derives utility from both leisure and the consumption of goods (purchased with earnings from paid work time). This utility is maximized over a specified time period subject to the prevailing budget constraint (the period may be one year, several years, or the remaining lifetime). Individual preferences are assumed to be stable during the specified period; in multi-period analysis, the utility functions are usually assumed to be intertemporally separable, i.e., that preferences during one period do not affect preferences in subsequent periods. Given these assumptions, numerous studies have examined the responses of individuals to observed changes in their budget constraint, especially their responses to changes in earnings (wage rate) and earnings-replacing income from OAI and PP benefits.

Any change in the wage rate generates a positive substitution effect and a negative income effect on the supply of work time. At the lower end of the earnings distribution, the substitution effect is stronger than the income effect, but at the upper end, the income effect is predominant. Nonwage income, by contrast, generates only an income effect; and since leisure time is a normal good (except perhaps for workaholics), an increase in nonwage income increases the demand for leisure time and curtails the supply of work time. However, an earnings-replacing income is a special form of nonwage income because it may generate both income and substitution effects on labor supply. The acceptance of earnings-replacing income imposes restrictions on earnings, and the age at which such income is accepted for the first time may affect the amount of income to be received over the remaining lifetime.[6]

Within some age-specific ranges, the annual benefit-amount increases with the age of acceptance. An analysis which is confined to the spot labor supply would conclude that this credit for delayed benefit acceptance generates a substitution effect in favor of continued work; hence, the observed negative effect of such income on labor supply suggests that the income effect on an earnings-replacing income is stronger than its substitution effect. However, such a spot-analysis ignores the effect of fewer annual installments over the remaining lifetime; the actuarial adjustment is insufficient if, despite the increased level of annual OAI and PP benefits, the total income received over life decreases when acceptance of such income is postponed. This possibility has led to an analysis of the labor supply response to changes in earnings-replacing income over the entire remaining life; the Social Security wealth (SSW) and the wealth derived from employer-provided pension (PPW) are measured by the present discounted value of the income stream over the remaining lifetime. Any computed level of SSW and PPW depends on the selection of the discount rate (r);[7] and, given the discount rate, this level also depends on gender differences in the average length of life so that equal annual incomes at the same ages result in higher levels of SSW and PPW for women than for men. The majority of the studies focused on men and, therefore, did not have to consider gender differences in SSW and PPW.

In addition to discount rate and gender, the level of SSW and PPW can be affected by the age of first acceptance. If the increase in annual benefits is sufficient to compensate for fewer annual installments, the age of acceptance does not change SSW and PPW; in such a case, the annual amount of OAI and PP benefits is actuarially fair. Actuarially unfair annual benefits occur when the level of SSW and PPW is not invariant to the age of acceptance. If SSW and PPW increase with the age of acceptance, workers have an economic incentive to postpone benefit acceptance and continue to work. If SSW and PPW decrease with the age of acceptance, workers have an incentive to accept pension benefits without delay and abide by the imposed restrictions on earnings; the substitution effect reinforces the income or wealth effect of earnings-replacing income in favor of increased demand for leisure and decreased supply of work time.

Empirical findings determine whether SSW and PPW are age-neutral; and they also show the extent to which an unfair actuarial adjustment encourages or discourages continued work. Regression estimates have been based on separate equations for the decision to participate in the labor force and for the number of hours worked by participants. This distinction facilitates the estimation procedure; but it introduces a bias because both the participation equation and the conditional labor-supply equation are derived from the same theoretical model of the individual's choice between work time and leisure time subject to the budget constraint.[8] Heckman (1974 and 1980) shows how the conditional labor supply has to be adjusted for differences between participants and nonparticipants. Most studies estimate a reduced-form participation equation and do not estimate the number of hours worked conditional on participation in the labor force; thus they avoid the problem of adjusting the conditional labor supply for the sample selection bias.[9]

The concept of retirement has been translated into several different measures. One commonly acceptable definition of retirement is withdrawal from the labor market with no intention of reentry. Another definition reflects the close association between the acceptance of an earnings-replacing income and the curtailment of labor supply; it focuses on the age at which OAI and PP income is accepted for the first time and on whether such acceptance is followed by withdrawal from the labor market. Other definitions view retirement as a separation from primary career employment or from the job held at age 55 (the age at which a worker is being characterized as an older worker). Thus, some definitions of retirement allow for part-time work (partial retirement), and some definitions even allow for full-time work in a secondary job, i.e., in a job which is regarded as temporary, provides no fringe benefits, and is characterized by a flat age-earnings profile. The effect of Social Security annual benefits or lifetime wealth on retirement (however defined) is far from clear-cut, as is evident from the studies discussed hereafter.

Social Security Work Disincentives

Several studies focus attention on the work disincentives generated by the income or wealth effect of OAI benefits which are available from age 62. Quinn (1977) demonstrates that eligibility for OAI and PP benefits reduces the labor force participation of white married men (aged 58 to 63 in April 1969) whereas the coefficient for the wage rate is not statistically significant. He concludes that the income effect of the available OAI and PP benefits constitute a strong factor in pulling eligible workers out of the labor market before age 65. Burtless and Moffitt (1984) define retirement to be a "discontinuous drop in labor supply" (p. 138) from full-time work to part-time work or no work. The frequency distribution of retirement ages thus defined has two peaks, a lower one at age 62 and a higher one at age 65. In their own words, "at age 62, relaxation of the liquidity constraints induces a surge of retirements" (p. 155).[10] The relaxation results from the ability, beginning at age 62, to dispose of the SSW which has been accumulating from the beginning of work life; the availability of this wealth encourages a drop in labor supply and early retirement.

The rules of the Social Security system have created an excess wealth for the present generation of beneficiaries, a wealth which eligible persons cannot enjoy unless they apply for OAI benefits. According to Pellechio, this wealth effect encourages workers to retire early in order to maximize the utility derived from the leisure which this excess wealth can provide. Pellechio (1979, 1981) measures excess wealth as the difference between the level of SSW and the present value of payroll taxes paid during worklife (this excess will disappear for future retirees). Pellechio's study (1978a) of married men in 1972 determines that SSW has no effect on the probability of exit from the labor market at ages 60 to 61 because SSW cannot be consumed before age 62; but SSW levels increase the probability of retirement after age 61 whereas the wage rate reduces the probability of retirement (wife's wage rate is held constant). Pellechio (1981) shows that additions to SSW because of continued work reduce the probability of retirement, but their effect is stronger for men age 62 to 64 than for men age 65 to 70.[11] He concludes that, although not all the rules of the Social Security system encourage early retirement, some of its rules are not age-neutral and, therefore, distort labor supply choices. In his view, a government pension system should have the same effect at all ages and should not influence the choice between work and retirement by tilting the retirement decision either toward younger or older ages.

A more focused case against the age-effect of the Social Security rules is made by Burkhauser (1977, 1980). Confining his studies to men and assuming a positive discount rate, Burkhauser shows that SSW at age 62 is higher than SSW at older ages. He concludes that this age nonneutrality provides a strong economic incentive to claim OAI benefits as early as possible and curtail earnings (and work) in order to avoid the benefit-loss imposed by the Social Security earnings test. Thus, Social Security rules generate not only an income or wealth effect but also a substitution effect in favor of reduced labor supply and increased demand for leisure. Although the probability of claiming OAI benefits at age 62 decreases when earnings-levels increase, the earnings of persons who postpone the acceptance of benefits have to be adjusted by the amount of lifetime benefits that are lost; the greater the potential loss of benefits, the lower the adjusted level of earnings and, therefore, the lower the price of time spent not working. This reduced price of leisure time encourages workers to increase their demand for leisure time and curtail their labor supply earlier than they otherwise would.

The Social Security system subjects beneficiaries to an earnings test; benefits are withheld at a rate of $1 for each $2 of earnings above a specified exempt amount (EA).[12] This test encourages beneficiaries to restrict their earnings to a level that is just below the exempt amount, as shown by Vroman (1972) and by Burtless and Moffitt (1984).[13] It may also explain the decision to work part-time.[14] Since EA is the same for all beneficiaries regardless of their wage rates, the amount of hours that can be worked without having benefits withheld is the inverse of the wage rate, or $H_0 = EA/W$, where H_0 denotes the number of hours at which a worker's earnings equal EA. When a worker's wage rate is adjusted for the benefit-withholding rate, the budget line is kinked at H_0 and, as Hanoch and Honig (1978) show, the labor-supply function is discontinuous. Most studies avoid this complication by estimating only a labor force participation equation. Yet, a few studies have estimated the supply of hours worked. Pellechio (1978b) as well as Burtless and Moffitt (1984) struggle with this complication. Hanoch and Honig (1983) estimate the hours worked by older workers eligible for and beneficiaries of OAI benefits, but they ignore the effect of the earnings test on the amount of hours supplied to the labor market.

Pellechio (1978b) states explicitly the formal conditions for working, given that the earnings test affects individual choices of the number of hours worked. He distinguishes four mutually exclusive choices: (1) earnings below EA, (2) earnings equal EA (at the kink), (3) earnings exceed EA and benefits are being withheld, and (4) earnings exceed EA but benefits are not withheld because they have been exhausted. The number of hours supplied to the labor market is not randomly distributed among these positions; rather, it depends on each individual's supply (reservation) wage in relation to his demand (market-offer) wage net of benefit losses. Pellechio's econometric estimates follow this quite elaborate theoretical design only partly. He concludes that removal of the earnings-test would have increased the labor supply of men age 65 to 70 in 1972 by an average of 151 hours per year.

Burtless and Moffitt (1984) view the labor supply of older workers as a continuum from no-work to full-time work, and they study the effect of Social Security rules on the age of retirement and on work during the first year after retirement (p. 151). Their unique contribution is the integration of two labor-supply decisions (usually kept separate) into a jointly estimated model: (1) at what age to retire, and (2) at what level to work after retirement. They use nonlinear maximum-likelihood estimates over several segments of the nonlinear budget constraint (not retired, retired and earning above EA, retired and earning equal or below EA, retired and having no earnings). The earnings test can account for the number of hours worked by working beneficiaries, but it does not explain why 80 percent of beneficiaries do not work, except if the fixed costs of working and the limited number of part-time jobs lead beneficiaries to forgo earnings below EA. The authors conclude that removal of the earnings test will add 10.6 hours per week to the number of hours worked by workers who are affected by the earnings test (p. 162). But this effect is diluted because only 20 percent of all beneficiaries work and only 10 percent are affected by the earnings-test; spread over all beneficiaries, in their first year of retirement, the removal of the earnings test increases hours of work from 3.2 to 4.2 hours per week. The effect of the earnings test on labor supply decreases with age because, as beneficiaries age, they are less likely to work.

Social Security Work Disincentives Reconsidered

These studies emphasize that Social Security rules have been responsible for the reduction in work and for the tendency toward early retirement. This conclusion is based on: (1) the wealth effect or the excess wealth effect and the relaxation of the liquidity constraint when accumulated wealth can be used for consumption, and (2) the substitution effect against work which results from an insufficient actuarial adjustment and from the restrictions on earnings by beneficiaries. Other studies agree that the Social Security rules are not age-neutral; but, in contrast, they point out that the Social Security rules have encouraged rather than discouraged continued work, at least until age 65.

The first study to make this case, by Gordon and Blinder (1980), shows that, for men age 58 to 67 during 1969–1973, SSW has had no effect on the probability of exit from the labor market. Rather, age per se increases the reservation wage, by 4 percent at ages 58 to 64 and by 6 percent at ages 65 to 67. Further, this study demonstrates that withdrawal from the labor force is the result of a job loss late in worklife, regardless of whether this loss is due to mandatory retirement rules, a bout of ill health or unemployment; late in worklife, the transition to another job is difficult and entails a considerable loss in wages.

Blinder, Gordon, and Wise (BGW)(1980) investigate the reason that SSW does not increase early retirement. They demonstrate how the Social Security provision for automatic benefit recomputation (ABR) encourages continued work. The earnings base for computing benefits, i.e., the average monthly earnings level (AME), is determined by the highest level of Social Security covered earnings during a predetermined number of years. Therefore, when earnings late in work life are higher than earlier earnings, continued work after age 61 can lead to higher levels of AME and higher annual benefits. BGW show this to be the case for the overwhelming majority of men eligible for OAI benefits in the early and mid-1970s. Further, they show that the loss in SSW due to postponed acceptance of benefits is more than offset by the gain in SSW due to continued work from age 62 to age 65, lifetime benefits are increased by the combination of increased AME and the actuarial adjustment (i.e., the increases in annual level of benefits when benefits are not accepted until age 65.[15] The gains in SSW have been reduced by the 1977 Amendment to the Social Security Act because this Amendment specifies that, effective in 1979, AIME replaces AME for every person born after 1916.[16] Gordon (1982) shows that, given the rules prevailing in 1981, the Social Security-generated work incentives ("wage subsidy" is his expression) continue to discourage retirement before age 65 by persons born before 1921. Thus, these studies strongly suggest that the Social Security system has not encouraged the present generation of retirees to stop working before age 65.

Moreover, Boaz (1985) shows that prospective beneficiaries, males and females, are less likely to file for OAI benefits at age 62 when, at age 61, they work full-time rather than part-time or not at all. For persons with earnings above the specified EA level, the opportunity cost of accepting benefits at age 62 or at any age before 65 equals the sum of the forgone earnings specified by the earnings test and the foregone earnings-induced increases in SSW due to the ABR provision. This opportunity cost serves as a deterrent to the accepting benefits at age 62. Boaz determines that, under the rules that prevailed in the early and mid-1970s, the financial disincentives which the Social Security system generated against acceptance of OAI benefits at age 62 outweighed the financial incentives it generated in favor of such acceptance. Hence, on balance, the Social Security system has not encouraged workers under age 65 to accept OAI benefits if such acceptance means giving up earnings. Applicants for permanently reduced annual benefits are likely to be men and women who, for reasons unrelated to Social Security rules, do not have much (if any) earnings to give up. In other words, the Social Security system is more likely to accommodate applicants who have already had a drop in earnings than to encourage full-time workers to curtail their labor supply before age 65 in order to accept reduced OAI benefits.[17]

Data from many studies suggest that the effect of earnings offsets the effect of SSW on the probability of retirement. For example, the studies by Burkhauser (1977, 1980) and by Pellechio (1978a) can be interpreted in this manner, although the authors emphasized the effect of SSW on the acceptance of OAI benefits at age 62 or on the withdrawal from the labor market. Further, Clark, Johnson, and McDermed (1980) examine the labor force participation of married men (age 58 to 67 during 1969–1973) as a joint family decision, and they determine that husbands' own wage rate and SSW raise the probability of males' labor force participation. They conclude that: "These findings imply that the market orientation that produces large Social Security benefits reduces the tendency toward early retirement but may be associated with greater retirement rates at approximately age 65" (p. 13). In addition, Fields and Mitchell (1984a) and Mitchell and Fields (1984) show that the age of retirement (which they define as the age of separation from primary employment) depends not only on the level of the anticipated stream of earnings and benefits for the remaining lifetime but also on the growth of this income stream due to continued work. They find that the age of retirement decreases with the level (at age 60) of the total income stream, and it increases when earnings and earnings-replacing income are expected to grow as a result of continued work; or, to put it differently, the wealth effect in favor of early retirement is more than offset by the substitution effect of changes in earnings that favor continued work. These results hold for their sample of workers who belong to different employer-provided pension plans despite considerable differences in plan-specific benefit formulas, suggesting that gains in money income provide for economic incentives that are strong enough to motivate older workers to continue work.

It appears that earnings levels and earnings growth play an important role in determining when workers retire. Studies which emphasize the effect of both earnings and benefits on labor market behavior have concluded that, on balance, the provisions of the Social Security system do not encourage workers to walk away from their primary jobs and retire before age 65. But studies which stress the effect of benefits and disregard the effect of earnings on labor market behavior have concluded that Social Security rules encourage workers to curtail their labor supply in order to avoid losses of lifetime benefits, a conclusion which fails to account for the withdrawal from the labor market of men who are too young and not disabled enough to qualify for any Social Security benefits. An alternative hypothesis might suggest that early retirement is due to an age-based loss of earnings. The next section examines the possible effects of such an earnings loss on the labor market behavior of older workers approaching retirement. Specifically, it examines whether employers' economic interests dictate the separation of older employees from their primary job before the age of normal retirement and whether the early separation from their career job leads workers to retire at a relatively young age.

Effects of Labor Market Conditions on the Timing of Retirement by Older Workers

Economic theory specifies that employers pay each employee the value of his marginal product. Hence, employers would have no economic incentive to terminate older workers because of age or length of company service. Therefore, if workers retire, their labor market behavior has to be ascribed to their own preferences in response to the availability of employer-provided pensions and Social Security benefits. However, this conclusion does not explain why men drop out of the labor force and retire at a time when they do not receive income from an employer-provided pension and do not qualify for Social Security benefits. In other words, if the timing of retirement is completely discretionary on the part of a worker, it would be surprising that men with low levels of nonwage income retire before they are old enough to be eligible for OAI benefits.

It is well known that wage growth is positively associated with duration of company service or seniority. The marginal productivity theory of demand for workers suggests that a seniority-related wage growth is the result of seniority-related increases in productivity. As explained by the theory of investment in human capital, seniority-based wage growth is a return to firm-specific investment in human capital (Mincer and Jovanovic, 1981). However, Medoff and Abraham (1980, 1981a) demonstrate from personnel records that earnings growth is a reward for longevity without commensurate increases in productivity. Earnings growth is positively associated with the duration of company service, but length of service is not positively associated with the importance and difficulty of the performed tasks.

Lazear (1981) explains that wage growth in excess of productivity growth late in work life is a return to excess productivity growth over wage growth earlier in work life. He views this arrangement as an incentive scheme designed to spur workers to a maximum effort over the duration of their implicit employment contract; workers maximize effort, especially during the early part of their work life, in order to be retained and reap the reward of excess earnings growth over productivity growth in the later years of their work life. Such an incentive scheme explains the widely observed personnel policies of age-related mandatory retirement, age- and seniority-related early-pension options, and the seniority-related protection against involuntary layoffs and terminations before the age of mandatory retirement.

The mandatory retirement provisions appear to be paradoxical in the context of both marginal productivity theory and human capital theory. It is difficult to explain why presumably the most productive workers, as evidenced by their steep age-earnings profiles, would be subject to a forced separation from their career jobs when they reach an arbitrarily specified age. Lazear's (1979) explanation shows that mandatory retirement is consistent with his reinterpretation of the marginal productivity theory. The equality between wage rates and the value of marginal product is not necessarily contemporaneous but applies to the entire duration of the implicit long-term employment contract. When worker's productivity cannot be easily monitored, the incentive scheme of deferred compensation assures maximum worker productivity over the entire work life. Older workers whose earnings exceed the value of their marginal product late in work life have an incentive to continue work under such favorable employment conditions. Mandatory retirement provisions signal the expiration of this implicit contract at the time that the present value of earnings equals the present value of the worker's marginal product over the entire duration of the implicit contract. Lazear's empirical findings confirm his hypothesis that mandatory retirement applies to the most favored workers. The probability that a worker is subject to mandatory retirement is higher (1) for white males than for nonwhites and females, (2) for union workers than for nonunion workers, and (3) for workers covered by an employer-provided pension than for workers without such pensions; and this probability increases with the level of schooling, the length of company service, and the rate of wage growth.

The excess of compensation over productivity which is positively associated with seniority explains why employers would have an economic incentive to terminate their long-tenured employees before the age of mandatory retirement. Lazear (1982) suggests that employers have used their defined-benefit pension plans to buy out the remaining years of an implicit contract. Employers can tilt the present value of pensions toward their early acceptance by specifying pension-formulas that reduce PPW with the age of acceptance, so that any delay in pension acceptance entails a loss in lifetime pension income.[18] He tests this hypothesis by computing PPW on the basis of the formulae reported by the pension plans of the large corporations surveyed by Bankers Trust in 1975; and he shows that PPW decreases steadily with the acceptance-age during the ten years preceding the age of mandatory retirement.[19] Lazear concludes that the personnel policy of large corporations is designed to persuade their older and senior employees to quit before the age of mandatory retirement. These large corporations do not fire their senior workers because such an action would be perceived by all employees as breach of contract and would make it difficult to hire junior workers under a similar incentive scheme.

The tilt of PPW in favor of an early voluntary separation and the positive association between employer-provided pensions and mandatory retirement rules, prompted Burkhauser and Quinn (1983) to examine the extent to which separation from primary employment could be attributed to pension rules rather than to explicit mandatory retirement provisions. They examined the labor market behavior of men ages 62 to 64 who were subject to mandatory retirement from the jobs at which they had been working in April 1973. It can be deduced from their table 3 (col. 1) that two years later at ages 64 to 66, 25 percent of these men were separated from their primary employment and had withdrawn from the labor market because of mandatory retirement rules. In other words, a nonnegligible proportion of workers subject to mandatory retirement might have continued to work beyond the specified age of mandatory retirement. Thus, although PPW decreases with age and although this decrease induces early voluntary separation from primary employment, employers cannot be sure that what they regard as a timely separation of their older employees will occur without explicit rules about mandatory retirement.

Older workers who withdraw from the labor market after opting for an early pension can be viewed as voluntary early retirees if they have an alternative choice of continuing to work for their primary employer. However, some older workers do not have such a choice, especially if they are discharged from their primary employment without income from an employer-provided pension. Medoff and Abraham (1981b) conclude from their survey of personnel policies that the so-called implicit employment contract is much less binding than the explicit (union) contract. The incentive scheme for deferred compensation implies that the personnel policy of inverse-seniority in ordering layoffs and terminations is designed to protect workers against the loss of compensation due to them late in work life. Yet, workers who have no explicit employment contract are much more likely to be laid off or terminated without regard for seniority rules than workers protected by a union contract; managerial and professional employees have much less seniority-related protection than other salaried employees, and all salaried employees have much less seniority-related protection than hourly wage workers.

Seniority-related wage growth, which leads to higher earnings for older (senior) workers than for younger (junior) workers of comparable skills, can explain why older workers encounter difficulties in finding reemployment late in work life. A new employer would be reluctant to employ such a worker at the wage paid by the previous employer when such a wage exceeds the value of current productivity. Moreover, at each wage rate, an employer incurs age-related employment costs when the employer provides such fringe-benefits as defined-benefit pensions and group health insurance.[20] Diamond and Hausman (1984) show that men over age 44 who have been discharged from their primary job cannot easily find reemployment; the duration of unemployment-spells increases with age as does the proportion of men who withdraw from the labor market. They determine that, during 1966–1978, the probability of retirement increased with the length of the unemployment spells in addition to the distinct and separate effects of age, health-status, and eligibility for Social Security benefits. They conclude that older workers who are separated from their primary jobs when they are too young to qualify for OAI benefits suffer a considerable income loss; for such men, any increase in the age of eligibility for OAI benefits increases financial hardship.

Since employers have an economic incentive not to retain their older employees, Boaz (1986) examines the relationship between employment conditions late in work life and early retirement. She shows that men who are too young to qualify for Social Security benefits are more likely to drop out of the work force if they had spent their work life as employees rather than as self-employed, and if they have been separated from their primary employment and do not have an alternative full-time job. She also shows that when these men are separated from primary employment without receiving income from an employer provided pension, their income is about half the income of pensioners. Early retirement under such conditions is likely to be a reaction to diminished employment opportunities following the separation from primary career employment before the age of normal retirement.

Self-employed men are more likely to continue work and delay retirement than wage-and-salary workers. There is evidence that some older workers postpone retirement by switching to self-employment late in work life; the longitudinal Retirement History Survey shows that the proportion of self-employed men increases with age. Fuchs (1982) examines the characteristics of older workers who switch to self-employment late in work life; and he also investigates whether self-employed men continue to work when otherwise similar employees stop working. Switching to self-employment depends very much on past experience and skills; it is more likely for men who, as employees, were managers, professionals, and salesmen than for men in clerical and blue-collar occupations.[21] Also, switches to self-employment are more likely for men who, as employees, were used to a flexible work-time schedule. For both recent switchers and long-timers, self-employment increases the probability of continued work relative to wage and salary employment.[22] In other words, when labor market conditions encourage continued work, men who have the required experience and skill are likely to continue work as self-employed. Self-employed workers stop working at more advanced age than employees, but the probability of continued work as a self-employed worker decreases with age and with the availability of earnings-replacing incomes.

Conclusion

The available research on labor market behavior of older workers approaching retirement is based on data from the mid-1960s to the late 1970s. The studies which emphasized the effect of benefits on the decision to retire attributed the trend toward early retirement to the rules of the Social Security system. These studies had a considerable influence on shaping the rule-changes that were specified by the 1983 Amendments to the Social Security Act. (Studies with a 1983 or 1984 publication date were circulating as working papers before 1983). Specifically, these Amendments stipulate a gradual increase in the age of entitlement to full annual benefits and a gradual increase in the credit for delayed retirement. When these rule changes are fully implemented, they are expected to remove the economic disincentives to continued work and to raise the age of retirement because, by comparison with current rules, they reduce the level of SSW and, at this lower level, provide for an approximately fair actuarial adjustment of benefits accepted anytime between ages 62 and 70.[23]

Three studies independently examined how lower SSW and age-neutral annual benefits would have changed the age of retirement in the late 1970s or early 1980s. Two studies estimate the effect on the retirement age of: (1) increasing the age of entitlement to full benefits from 65 to 68 and (2) lowering the reduction factor for benefits accepted at age 62 from 80 percent to 60 percent of full benefits. Fields and Mitchell (1984b, tables 10.2 and 10.4) show that if these changes were in effect during 1982, they would have lowered SSW gradually with the age of acceptance (from a reduction of 25 percent at age 62 to a reduction of 9 percent at age 68. Burtless and Moffitt (1984) estimate the level of SSW to be lower by 15–17 percent if these changes were in effect in 1978. Yet, despite such large reductions in SSW, the average age of retirement would have increased only slightly, by 1.6 months according to Fields and Mitchell, and by at most 4.5 months according to Burtless and Moffitt. Further, Fields and Mitchell examine the effect of other changes; they determine that: (1) a substantial increase in the credit for delayed retirement (from 3 percent to 6.67 percent for each year that benefit acceptance is postponed between ages 65 and 68 has almost no effect on the average age of retirement, and (2) a substantial decrease in benefits accepted at age 62 (from 80 percent to 55 percent of full benefits at age 65) raises the average age of retirement only by three months. Similarly, Burtless and Moffitt show that actuarially fair annual benefits raise the average age of retirement by only 4.5 months. A third study, by Gustman and Steinmeier (1985 and 1983) compares the effects of the rules specified by the 1983 and the 1977 Amendments to the Social Security Act; the 1983 rules raise the average age of retirement from full-time work from 62.3 to 62.5, and the average age of retirement from all work from 63.4 to 63.7 (Gustman and Steinmeier, 1983, table B.1)

The results from these studies demonstrate that the age of retirement is not sensitive to substantial changes in the level of SSW and in the actuarial adjustment of annual benefits. Or to put it differently, if the removal of Social Security work dis-incentives and the strengthening of the incentives for delayed retirement raise the retirement age only very slightly, it is unlikely that Social Security rules are responsible for the observed trend toward early retirement. This conclusion can also be derived from the studies which emphasize the effects of both pension benefits and earnings on the labor market behavior of older workers. Moreover, this conclusion is consistent with studies which show that employers have an economic incentive to separate their senior workers from primary employment, and induce such a separation several years before workers are eligible for Social Security benefits or reach the age of normal retirement. The separation from primary employment may entail a substantial and irreversible loss of earnings, and the timing of this loss is likely to determine when workers retire. Some separated workers may avoid or mitigate this loss because they have the skills and experience to switch to self-employment and continue work; others, who lack the skills for self-employment and encounter difficulties in finding steady full-time work as employees, may decide to withdraw from the labor market. When they reach the age of entitlement to Social Security benefits, they are likely to claim benefits, and the Social Security system will accommodate them by replacing part of their lost earnings with permanently reduced annual benefits.

The evidence from the 1970s suggests that, even under the current rules, the Social Security system does not, on balance, encourage older workers to walk away from their primary jobs and forego earnings in order to accept permanently reduced annual benefits before age 65. Yet, the trend toward acceptance of reduced benefits has continued unabated. It is not likely to be halted or reversed unless the trend toward the age-related decline in labor force participation is reversed. The trend toward early withdrawal from the workforce is not likely to be halted and reversed without an improvement of the labor market conditions facing older workers. Moreover, the legislated changes in the Social Security system that are specified by the 1983 Amendments as remedies for the observed labor market behavior are not likely to reverse the current trend toward early acceptance of Social Security benefits if, as some of the evidence shows, the observed labor market behavior stems from diminished employment opportunities for older workers.

Notes

1. For example, the level of newly awarded benefits (in constant 1967 prices) increased by 2.2 percent annually during 1965–1970, by 5.6 percent annually during

1970–1975, and by 3.5 percent per year during 1975–1977 (*Annual Statistical Supplement to the Social Security Bulletin*, 1965, table 65; 1970, table 70; 1975, table 67; 1977, table 64). For persons age 55–59, the rate of benefit-awards per 100,000 insured workers who were not beneficiaries increased at an annual rate of 3.3 percent during 1967–1970, and 9.5 percent during 1970–1974 (Lando and Krute, 1976).

2. The reduction factor is 5/9 of one percent for each month that benefits are accepted prior to age 65; from age 65 to age 69, benefits are increased by ¼ of one percent for each month that benefit acceptance is delayed.

3. Hatch (1982) examines the information available from the 1979 Level of Benefits (LOB) survey which represents 21 million workers out of 38.6 million workers over age 25 who were covered by employer-provided pensions in the private sector. She found that 73 percent were covered by pension plans that offered the option of pension acceptance at age 55 and 19 percent were covered by plans which offered such an option at age 60 (p. 52). Thus, the early pension option appears to be the rule rather than the exception among large pension plans which cover the majority of workers eligible for a pension upon separation from their primary employment.

4. Examples of hazardous professions are the military, firefighters, police and other law-enforcement personnel. In these professions, the declining physical fitness, which is expected with age, increases the risk to health and life.

5. For example, during periods of reduction-in-force (RIF), the Federal government has encouraged departure from the civil service as early as age 50 for workers with 20 years of civil service employment and has encouraged departure even at younger ages for employees with 25 years of civil service employment.

6. Social Security beneficiaries are subject to withholding of benefits if earnings exceed the "exempt amount" specified by the earnings-test. Acceptors of employer-provided pensions cannot continue to work for the employer who provides the pension. Such restrictions lead OAI beneficiaries and pension acceptors to give up full-time work and often result in complete withdrawal from the labor market.

7. For example, given that OAI benefits at age 62 are equal to 80 percent of OAI benefits at age 65, and given that the average life expectancy of males is 15 years at age 62 and 12 years at age 65, SSW is the same at age 65 as at age 62 if $r = 0$, 5.5 percent lower if $r = 3$ percent, and 8.1 percent if $r = 5$ percent.

8. Nonparticipation is the special case where the budget constaint-line is tangent to the set of indifference curves at zero hours of work; participation is the case where the hours worked are positive at the point of tangency. (The indifference curves represent various combinations of total time and income.) The longer the time over which labor-force participation is measured, the greater the probability of participation, e.g., participation during a period of one year is more likely than participation during a week. Usually, the time period considered is limited to one year, although theoretically, participation during lifetime is a relevant concept for analysis.

9. Nonparticipants (for whom hours of work and wage rates are not observed) differ systematically from participants; hence, the practice of imputing wages and hours of work based on the characteristics of participants leads to a specification error and to biased regression coefficients. This bias is referred to as sample selection or selectivity bias.

10. The liquidity constraint is the result of the inability of prospective beneficiaries to consume their accumulated SSW before age 62 because, in the existing

imperfect capital market, they cannot use future SSW as collateral for borrowing and for consumption before they reach the age of eligibility.

11. The effect of continued work on raising the earnings base for computing OAI benefits was brought to the attention of researchers by Blinder, Gordon, and Wise (1980). Their study is discussed below in subsection B.

12. In 1986, EA = $5,760 for persons under age 65 and EA = $7,800 for persons age 65 and older.

13. Lingg (1980) shows that, of all men age 65–71 in 1977 and eligible for benefits, 15.3 percent had earnings in excess of the exempt amount.

14. Gustman and Steinmeier (1984) argue that part-time work is a form of partial retirement. In any given year, the proportion of partially retired men is small; but at least one-quarter of the men age 65–69 in April 1975 reported partial retirement some time between age 59 and age 69 (table 2). Honig and Hanoch (1985) show that partial retirement is a transitory short phase with a median duration of approximately 1.25 years (table 6).

15. Burkhauser and Turner (1980) and Burkhauser (1977, 1980) are directly challenged by BGW's study. Burkhauser and Turner (1981) agree that ABR (which they overlooked) encourages continued work but they disagree on the strength of this work incentive.

16. AIME is the average monthly earnings adjusted for changes over time in the wage index. Indexed earnings are less likely to be lower than nominal earnings after age 61; hence, increases in the earnings-loss after age 61 are likely to be small.

17. The level of foregone earnings as a determinant of benefit acceptance also explains why even women without spouses (e.g., respondents to the Retirement History Survey) are more likely than men to apply for early and permanently reduced benefits, although women expect to live longer than men and do not lose SSW by postponing benefit acceptance until age 65. On the average, women's earnings are lower than men's earnings and, therefore, their foregone earnings are lower.

18. If employer-provided pension plans were strictly designed to be plans for tax-deferred savings, PPW would be age-neutral.

19. Similarly, in a study based for 2,342 defined-benefit plans (from the BLS Level of Benefits Survey), Kotlikoff and Wise (1984) show that substantial reductions of pension accruals occur at plan-specified ages of early and normal retirement, and that such changes decrease the level of total compensation from continued work in primary employment.

20. Barnow and Ehrenberg (1979, tables Ia, IIa, IIb) show that the costs to employers of defined-benefit pensions increase with the age composition (as distinct from the tenure composition) of their work force. Similarly, premiums for group health insurance also increase with the age composition of the work force because their level depends on utilization of medical services.

21. Quantitatively, the average probability of switching between 1969 and 1971 or between 1971 and 1973 is .04; but the predicted probability of switching by managers, professionals, salesmen and other workers with some previous experience in self-employment is .52 if such men do not receive pension income, and it is .003 for blue collar workers who are working a regular 40-hour week and are eligible for employer-provided pension upon retirement from their primary employment. See Fuchs (1982), p. 350.

22. During 1969–1973, self-employment of men age 58 to 63 in April 1969 increased the probability of continued work relative to wage and salary employment from .729 to .805.

23. The 1983 Amendments provide for a gradual increase in the age of entitlement to full benefits for all persons born after 1937, so that the age at which full benefits can be received is raised from 65 to 66 in 2009 and to 67 in 2027. The minimum age of benefit acceptance is unchanged; at age 62, however, the reduction factor, which is currently 80 percent of full benefits, is gradually lowered to 70 percent of full benefits for persons born in 1960 or thereafter. Further, the credit for delayed retirement, which is currently 3 percent per year between ages 65 and 70, is gradually raised (over an eighteen year period) to 8 percent per year for all persons born after 1924. And beginning in 1990, the earnings test is changed for beneficiaries who work after reaching the age of entitlement to full benefits; the rate at which benefits are withheld will be lowered from 50 to 33 cents for each dollar of earnings above the exempt amount (Svahn and Ross, 1983).

Bibliography

Barnow, B.S. and R.G. Ehrenberg. (1979). "The Costs of Defined Benefit Plans and Firm Adjustment," *The Quarterly Journal of Economics* (93), November, pp. 523–540.

Blinder, A.S., R.H. Gordon and D.E. Wise. (1980). "Reconsidering the Work-Disincentive Effects of Social Security," *National Tax Journal* (33), December, pp. 431–443.

———, ———, and ———. (1981). "Rhetoric and Reality in Social Security Analysis—A Rejoinder," *National Tax Journal* (34), December, pp. 473–478.

Boaz, R.F. (1985). "The Opportunity Cost of an Early Acceptance of Social Security Benefits" (unpublished).

———. (1986). "Early Withdrawal from the Labor Force: Only Pension Pull or Also Labor-Market Push?" (unpublished).

Burkhauser, R.V. (1980, 1977). "The Early Acceptance of Social Security: An Asset-Maximization Approach," *Industrial and Labor Relations Review* (33), July, pp. 484–492. (An expanded version of this article is available in a 1977 discussion paper, #463-77, Institute of Research on Poverty, University of Wisconsin-Madison).

——— and J. Turner. (1980). "The Effects of Pensions through Life," in R.L. Clark, ed., *Retirement Policy in an Aging Society* (Durham, NC: Duke University Press), pp. 128–142.

——— and ———. (1981). "Can Twenty-Five Million Americans Be Wrong?—A Response to Blinder, Gordon and Wise," *National Tax Journal* (34), December, pp. 467–472.

——— and J.F. Quinn. (1983). "Is Mandatory Retirement Overrated? Evidence from the 1970s," *The Journal of Human Resources* (18), Summer, pp. 337–358.

Burtless, G. and R.A. Moffitt. (1984). "The Effect of Social Security on the Labor Supply of the Aged," in H.J. Aaron and G. Burtless, eds., *Retirement and Economic Behavior* (Washington, DC: The Brookings Institution), pp. 135–171.

Chirikos, T.N. and G. Nestel. (1981). "Impairment and Labor Market Outcomes: A Cross-Sectional and Longitudinal Analysis," in H.S. Parnes, ed., *Work and Retirement: A Longitudinal Study of Men* (Cambridge, MA: MIT Press), chapter 4.

Clark, R.L., T. Johnson and A.A. McDermed. (1980). "Allocation of Time and Resources by Married Couples Approaching Retirement," *Social Security Bulletin* (43), April, pp. 3–16.

Diamond, P.A. and J.A. Hausman. (1984). "The Retirement and Unemployment Behavior of Older Men," in H.J. Aaron and G. Burtless, eds., *Retirement and Economic Behavior* (Washington, DC: The Brookings Institution), pp. 97–132.

Fields, G.S. and O.S. Mitchell. (1984a). "Economic Determinants of the Optimal Retirement Age: An Empirical Investigation," *The Journal of Human Resources* (19), Spring, pp. 245–262.

———— and ————. (1984b). *Retirement, Pensions and Social Security* (Cambridge, MA: MIT Press).

Freeman, R.B. (1979). "The Effects of Demographic Factors on Age-Earnings Profiles," *The Journal of Human Resources* (14), Summer, pp. 289–318.

Fuchs, V.R. (1982). "Self-Employment and Labor Force Participation of Older Males," *The Journal of Human Resources* (17), Summer, pp. 339–358.

Gordon, R.H. and A.S. Blinder. (1980). "Market Wages, Reservation Wages, and Retirement Decisions," *Journal of Public Economics* (14), October, pp. 277–308.

————. (1982). "Social Security and Labor Supply Incentives," National Bureau of Economic Research, Working Paper No. 986.

Gustman, A.L. and T.L. Steinmeier. (1985, 1983). "The 1983 Social Security Reforms and Labor Supply Adjustments of Older Individuals in the Long Run," *Journal of Labor Economics* (3), April, pp. 237–253, and an expanded version of this article in National Bureau of Economic Research Working Paper No. 1212.

———— and ————. (1984). "Partial Retirement and the Analysis of Retirement Behavior," *Industrial and Labor Relations Review* (37), July, pp. 403–415.

Hanoch, G. and M. Honig. (1978). "The Labor Supply Curve under Income Maintenance Programs," *Journal of Public Economics* (9), February, pp. 1–16.

————and————. (1983). "Retirement, Wages, and Labor Supply of the Elderly," *Journal of Labor Economics* (1), April, pp. 131–151.

Hatch, S.P. (1982). "Pension Plan Provisions That Directly Affect Retirement-Age Choice," in *Financial Retirement Incentives in Private Pension Plans* (Washington, DC: The Urban Institute), chapter 2.

Heckman, J.J. (1974). "Shadow Prices, Market Wages, and Labor Supply," *Econometrica* (42), July, pp. 679–694.

————. (1980). "Sample Selection Bias as a Specification Error," in J.P. Smith, ed., *Female Labor Supply* (Princeton, NJ: Princeton University Press), pp. 206–248.

Honig, M. and G. Hanoch. (1985). "Partial Retirement as a Separate Mode of Retirement Behavior," *The Journal of Human Resources* (20), Winter, pp. 21–46.

Kotlikoff, L.J. and D.A. Wise, (1984). "The Incentive Effects of Private Pension Plans," National Bureau of Economic Research Working Paper No. 1510.

Lando, M.E. and A. Krute. (1976). "The Growth of Observed Disability Incidence Rates, 1967–1974," paper presented at the 104th Annual Meeting of the American Public Health Association, October.

Lazear, E.P. (1979). "Why is There Mandatory Retirement?" *Journal of Political Economy* (87), December, pp. 1261–1284.

———. (1981). "Agency, Earnings Profiles, Productivity and Hours Restrictions," *The American Economic Review* (71), December, pp. 606–620.

———. (1982). "Severance Pay, Pensions and Efficient Mobility," National Bureau of Economic Research, Working Paper No. 854.

Lingg, B.A. (1980). "Beneficiaries Affected by the Annual Earnings Test in 1977," *Social Security Bulletin* (43), December, pp. 3–15.

Medoff, J.L. and K.G. Abraham. (1980). "Experience, Performance, and Earnings," The Quarterly Journal of Economics (95), November, pp. 703–736.

——— and ———. (1981a). "Are Those Paid More Really More Productive? The Case of Experience," *The Journal of Human Resources* (16), Spring, pp. 186–216.

——— and ———. (1981b). "Involuntary Terminations Under Explicit and Implicit Contracts," Harvard University, Working Paper No. 815.

Meier, E.L. and C.C. Dittmar. (1980). "Variety of Retirement Ages," Staff Working Paper, The President's Commission on Pension Policy (Washington, DC), October.

Mincer, J. and B. Jovanovic. (1981). "Labor Mobility and Wages," in S. Rosen, ed., *Studies in Labor Markets* (Chicago, IL: University of Chicago Press), pp. 21–63.

Mitchell, O.S. and G.S. Fields. (1984). "The Economics of Retirement Behavior," *Journal of Labor Economics* (2), January, pp. 84–105.

Parsons, D.O. (1980). "The Decline in Labor Force Participation of Prime Age Males," *Journal of Political Economy* (88), February, pp. 117–134.

———. (1982). "The Male Labour Force Participation Decision: Health, Reported Health and Economic Incentives," *Economica* (49), February, pp. 81–91.

Pellechio, A.J. (1978a). "The Effect of Social Security on Retirement," National Bureau of Economic Research, Working Paper No. 260.

———. (1978b). "The Social Security Earnings Test, Labor Supply Distortions, and Forgone Payroll Tax Revenue," National Bureau of Economic Research, Working Paper No. 272.

———. (1979). "Social Security Financing and Retirement Behavior," *American Economic Review* (69), May, pp. 284–287.

———. (1981). "Social Security and the Decision to Retire," National Bureau of Economic Research, Working Paper No. 734.

Quinn, J.F. (1977). "Microeconomic Determinants of Early Retirement: A Cross-Sectional View of White Married Men," *The Journal of Human Resources* (12), Summer, pp. 329–346.

Rogers, G.T. (1981). "Vesting of Private Pension Benefits in 1979 and Changes from 1972," *Social Security Bulletin* (44), July, pp. 12–29.

Russell, L.B. (1982). *The Baby Boom Generation and the Economy,* (Washington, DC: The Brookings Institution).

Svahn, J.A. and M. Ross. (1983). "Social Security Amendments of 1983: Legislative

History and Summary of Provisions," *Social Security Bulletin* (46), July, pp. 3–48.

Vroman, W. (1972). *Older Workers' Earnings and the 1965 Social Security Amendments,* Office of Research and Statistics, Social Security Administration, Research Report No. 38.

6
The Economic and Political Implications of a Phase-Out: A Summing Up

Charles W. Meyer

The economic case for compulsory social insurance is based in part on the theory of market failure. Markets for insurance against loss of earnings function imperfectly, and governmental intervention is prescribed as a corrective. Because government is not perfect either, the shortcomings of both arrangements must be considered.

Under some circumstances, a case may be made for constraining market outcomes. This may occur when market participants are deemed incapable of acting in their own best interest. Government may intervene, for example, by requiring us to provide for retirement through compulsory social insurance. Society, acting collectively through government, may decide to promote social welfare or other goals by redistributing income. Thus Social Security has a progressive benefit formula designed to provide higher relative (not absolute) returns to workers with lower earnings.

The case for a phase-out hinges in part on a rejection of market failure, paternalistic, and redistributive arguments for social insurance. In addition, Social Security is seen as a deterrent to saving, capital formation, and a freely functioning labor market. It is recognized that a phase-out will be costly for young workers who will pay for benefits to older persons without drawing benefits themselves. A key economic issue centers on whether the gains in output that are expected to accompany a closing down of the system will compensate the affected generation for their loss of benefits. Only if this is the case can young workers be expected to support a phase-out.

The Case for Social Insurance

The genius of Adam Smith was to recognize that markets can allocate scarce resources efficiently. Efficient allocation occurs when resources are allocated to their highest valued use. In a smoothly functioning market economy this is achieved by the interaction of large numbers of market participants acting in their own best interests. Smith, of course, recognized that markets do not always function efficiently. He was aware of the disruptive effect of monopoly, and he realized that some services, such as defense of the realm, can be supplied only by government.

Modern economics offers a greatly refined set of criteria for defining efficiency. These criteria in turn provide a means for identifying the causes of market failure. Market failure may be partial, as when monopolists fail to extend output to the point where price equals marginal cost or when, because of externalities, prices fail to reflect the full cost of production or the full benefit to society. Pollution is an example of the former; education and immunization are examples of the latter.

Markets may fail completely in the case of public goods. Examples are goods and services characterized by large numbers, nonrival consumption, and infeasibility of excluding nonpayers. Thus national defense or major flood control projects would not exist without government.[1]

Social Insurance and Market Failure

Economists who support compulsory social insurance base their support, at least in part, on the presence of market failure in markets for insurance. They conclude that private insurance markets will fail to insure the risks covered by Social Security efficiently, if at all. Governmental provision is therefore required. If they are correct, the case for phasing out Social Security is weakened considerably.

The purpose of insurance is to transfer risk from the insured to the insurer. If the probability distribution of outcomes can be determined, risks can be spread across a pool of policyholders. Premiums can be set so as to cover claims plus operating costs. If premiums accurately reflect risk, the market for insurance will function efficiently and there will be no market failure. Markets may fail if the probability distribution of outcomes cannot be determined or if it is not possible to allocate costs among the insured in a manner commensurate with risks. Insurers have devised means of adjusting for some of these difficulties by, for example, assigning individuals to different risk classes or limiting or denying coverage. These adjustments have extended the ability of insurance companies to offer protection, but they add to transactions costs and have failed in important ways to correct for market failure.

Social Security provides insurance against loss of earnings resulting from retirement, death of a worker, or disability. Two types of risk are covered, length of work life and longevity. As the essay by Rachel F. Boaz points out, the length of work life is influenced both by willingness and ability to work and by the availability of jobs for older workers. The risk of longevity complicates retirement planning, because a worker does not know how long he or she will be required to draw on accumulated savings for support. Social Security also insures against a portion of the cost of medical care for the elderly and disabled, the two groups with the highest medical expenses. Supporters of a phase-out, like Peter J. Ferrara, believe that private insurers can adequately cover all of these contingencies.[2] Economists who disagree cite various sources of market failure. These include moral hazard, adverse selection, uninsurable social risk, and excessive transactions costs.

Moral Hazard. When risk is transferred from the insured to the insurer, the incentive to avoid the insured event is altered. Reactive behavior by the insured may take two forms. One reaction is to commit fraud, as when a property owner commits arson in order to collect on fire insurance. Such behavior is illegal, and underwriting procedures are intended to filter out applicants deemed most likely to react in this manner. A second reaction is the economically rational change in behavior that occurs when another party bears a part or all of the cost of certain actions. For example, a building owner who purchases fire insurance is less likely to incur costs of repariing faulty wiring or removing combustible refuse than one who is self-insured. Both types of reaction are subsumed under the expression "moral hazard." The expression is obviously derived from the first, but it is the second that is most relevant for our purposes.[3]

It is clear that Social Security retirement benefits have allowed many workers in past and current retirement cohorts to leave the labor force. The incentive to retire has been strengthened by the large intergenerational transfers available to these workers. The tendency has been reinforced by the earnings test, inadequate actuarial adjustments for delayed retirement, and the lack of satisfactory employment opportunities for older workers who lose their jobs. Disability insurance has had a similar effect on workers with severe impairments.

Although these reactions are important when considering the effect of Social Security on labor supply, they are not germane to the issue of moral hazard as a source of market failure. In particular, the benefit windfalls to past and current retirement generations represent a governmental overriding of market forces, not a corrective for market inefficiencies.

If Social Security is phased out, private insurers would be called upon to insure against risks associated with longevity and premature death. Persons approaching retirement age could insure against longevity by converting some or all of their assets into an annuity. The insurer would pay them a predetermined amount, usually on a monthly basis, until they die. Risk of longevity would be spread across the population of annuitants. A younger worker with dependents could protect survivors against earnings loss by purchasing term life insurance. If the worker dies, the proceeds could be invested in income-earning assets whose yield would replace at least a portion of the lost earnings. Although it is conceivable that annuities and life insurance may cause some reactions that would affect life span, it seems unlikely that moral hazard is a significant source of market failure in these markets.

Disability insurance is more complicated, mainly because disability—the inability to work because of severe physical or mental impairment—is more difficult to define than death. An impairment that is disabling for one person may be merely a nuisance for another. The demands of the job and the ability to endure and overcome pain and other obstacles differ among individuals. The availability of an income stream from disability insurance will almost certainly affect the incentive to work or to seek rehabilitation or retraining. Insurers attempt to make risks more determinate and insurable by relating type and degree of impairments to levels of disability. This is a costly and litigious process, but it is necessary if work disincentives introduced by insurance are to be constrained.[4]

Private insurance covers a large share of the health care costs of the U.S. population, either through group plans or individual coverage. When third-party insurers cover a part or all of the cost of treatment, the economic incentives of both patients and suppliers of health care are altered considerably. This factor is frequently cited as the cause of the rapid rise in health-care costs that has continued unabated for decades. Private insurers and the government through Medicare and Medicaid have devised various means of limiting the costs of health care. The most common are arrangements that shift a part of the cost to patients. Deductibles place full cost of treatment below a specified dollar amount on the patient. This feature is intended to encourage patients to avoid treatment for trivial ailments and to reduce paper work. Coinsurance requires patients to share a fraction of the cost of insured treatment, giving patients and perhaps physicians an incentive to monitor costs. The patients share is usually 20 percent or less, however, making the effectiveness of coinsurance questionable. Another common practice is refusal of more than one insurer to reimburse a patient for a given treatment, even though the patient may have multiple coverage.

Insurers also attempt to control costs by monitoring the practices of suppliers of medical services and by limiting the maximum amount that they will pay for specified services and procedures. Recently, private group insurers have attempted to alter incentives to suppliers by contracting with health maintenance organizations and other group practitioners. Suppliers are paid a fixed annual fee per patient. This gives them an incentive to hold down costs by avoiding unnecessary treatment and by practicing preventive medicine.

Private insurers play a major role in providing medical insurance. They have developed a variety of institutional arrangements for controlling health-care costs. Thus one might reasonably conclude that private insurers could extend coverage to the medicare population without undue relaxation of the constraints on moral hazard.[5]

Adverse Selection. If everyone bought an annuity upon retirement, risks would be spread across the entire population. Benefit payments would be based on survival rates for the whole population. If private firms offered annuities of this type, the terms would appear most attractive to those who anticipate above-average longevity, and insurers would attract such persons in disproportionate numbers. If purchasers are on average correct in their expectations about longevity, as seems likely, insurance companies would be forced to adjust annuity prices upward. Annuities would become even less attractive especially for persons with less favorable survival expectations, and many would choose not to insure. This phenomenon is known as "adverse selection." Bad risks, in this case persons with long life expectancies, drive out good risks.

Adverse selection is a common feature in insurance markets. It also occurs in markets for disability, health, and life insurance. In order to achieve efficient allocation, insurers must segregate applicants into homogeneous risk categories. For example, life insurance companies screen applicants via physical examinations. Premiums rise with age and are lower for women than for men. Additional classifications are possible. Some companies offer lower rates to nonsmokers or nondrinkers. Life expectancies vary across racial and socioeconomic groups, and these factors could be reflected in premiums.

At some point the gains from risk homogeneity will be limited by the cost of further refinement. Efforts to allocate individuals to risk categories related to life style or occupation may be difficult or impossible to implement.

Public concern for fairness may be a more serious obstacle. For example, advocates of women's rights are exerting pressure for unisex pricing of annuities, life insurance, and automobile insurance. Their cause received a boost in 1983 when the U.S. Supreme Court ruled that employer-sponsored pension plans paying higher monthly benefits to men than to women are in violation of the 1964 Civil Rights Act.[6] Differences in premiums based on race encounter similar resistance.

Adverse selection has implications for a phase-out of Social Security, whether its cause is market failure or restrictions imposed on insurers in the name of fairness. If the desire is to spread risk across the entire population without driving good risks out of the market, this can be achieved in two ways. One is to assign all individuals to risk pools differentiated only by socially acceptable characteristics. For example, purchasers of life insurance or annuities might be differentiated only by age. All workers could then be required to buy life insurance, and all persons entering retirement could be required to buy annuities. Insurers would be required to sell policies to all applicants. Similar requirements could apply to disability insurance and medical insurance for the elderly and disabled. The mandatory coverage could be provided by firms in the private sector.

A second option would be for the government to offer voluntary insurance at premiums reflecting the same set of socially acceptable risk categories.

This would allow persons who are poor risks to purchase insurance at lower prices than would be available to them in segmented private markets. Private insurers could, of course, offer more attractive rates to good risks. The government insurance program might operate at a loss, but that is the price of combining voluntary purchases with societal standards of fairness.

High Transactions Costs. Supporters of a phase-out criticize Social Security because it forces workers to participate in a compulsory program that may not fit their individual needs. For example, single workers are forced to pay for survivor's insurance even though they may have no dependents. Working couples pay for spouse's benefits for single-earner couples. Workers cannot time their retirement savings over the life cycle. It would appear that a private system would be more efficient, because it would allow workers to allocate savings and purchases of insurance in accordance with their individual preferences.

Unfortunately, the flexibility that is characteristic of private insurance and investment markets is achieved at a rather high cost. For Social Security, administrative costs as a percentage of benefits are about 1 percent for old age and survivors insurance, 1.7 percent for hospital insurance, 3.2 percent for disability insurance, and 4 percent for supplementary medical insurance. In contrast, census data show that in 1982 commissions and other expenses of U.S. life insurance companies accounted for 36 percent of total disbursements and equaled 57 percent of payments to policyholders. Economists have long recognized that product differentiation carries a price.[7] With cost differentials of such magnitude, one can seriously question whether product differentiation and freedom of choice in these markets is worth the cost for most workers.

The data cited above refer to costs to suppliers. Consumers faced with responsibility for their own security needs must make complex choices that are costly in both time and resources. When decisions are made collectively, decision costs of individuals are reduced. Again, individual autonomy has its price. Additional concerns about individual decision making are examined below in the discussion of merit goods.

Of course it is not necessary to resort to compulsory social insurance to achieve economies in administrative and decision costs. These can be achieved through private pension plans. Employer and other group plans can be tailored to meet the needs of various groups, but they do not typically offer workers complete freedom of choice. In some cases they are as inflexible as Social Security, and they lack some of the advantages of a national system. In addition, private plans do not generally offer inflation protection to retired workers, nor do they offer the portability of Social Security, an important feature in a society in which job changes are frequent. Furthermore, as Rachel Boaz points out, private plans can be manipulated to encourage workers to retire early.

Social Risks. Private insurance works best when losses within the insured population are predictable. This is usually the case with individual risks of death, injury, or illness. Some risks, however, are social in nature. They affect large numbers of individuals, perhaps the entire population, and they are not predictable. An insurer may experience a loss on many or all of its policies and be unable to meet its contractual obligations. Risks of this type are called "social risks."

Macroeconomic occurrences such as inflation or deep and prolonged recession are examples of social risk that cannot be covered by private insurers. Private retirement annuities offer protection against risks of longevity, but private insurers cannot promise protection against erosion of purchasing power. Annuities cannot be indexed because private insurers cannot lock in constant *real* returns in their investment portfolios. Ferrara's sanguine view that accretion in the value of underlying assets will offer inflation protection is not consistent with the experience of the 1970s.[8]

Traditionally, retirement annuities have paid constant nominal benefit streams, although they can be adjusted to pay benefit streams that increase over time at a predetermined or ex ante rate. For a given initial purchase price, the benefit stream will be lower in early years and higher in later years than a constant nominal stream. This feature provides an added payoff to longevity. Its usefulness as an inflation hedge depends on the difference between anticipated and actual inflation rates.

Variable annuities, which tie benefits to the yield on an underlying asset portfolio, are another option available from private insurers. Market risks are transferred to the annuitant, but the insurer retains the risk associated with longevity.

Disability insurance is vulnerable to the impact of inflation and unemployment. The inflation risk is similar to that encountered in retirement annuities. Periods of high unemployment are likely to be accompanied by increases in applications for disability benefits, since workers with serious impairments are more likely to lose their jobs and fail to find new ones. High and prolonged unemployment can threaten the financial integrity of insurers. This was a common experience during the Great Depression.

The financing crises of 1977 and 1983 showed that Social Security is not immune to the effects of high inflation and a sluggish economy. The government, however, has greater flexibility than private insurers in adjusting to macroeconomic developments. The most important is its ability to tax. If indexing of benefits requires more revenue, payroll taxes can be increased or the general fund can be tapped. Thus a public system can provide inflation protection that private insurers cannot match.

In providing beneficiaries with inflation protection, government is insuring against a social risk for which it is largely responsible. Friedrich Hayek notes that by failing to maintain stable currencies, governments everywhere have robbed individuals of their retirement savings.[9] If governments were more responsible, publicly financed inflation protection would not be necessary. Since those who are no longer able to work are especially vulnerable, public demand for indexing of benefits is likely to persist. Of course without such protection, governments would be under stronger pressure to stabilize the price level.

Uninsurable social risks are not confined to economic factors. The retirement planning horizon is a long one, and major breakthroughs affecting longevity could impair the ability of individuals to provide for retirement. Both living expenses and cost of medical care could be affected. Improvements in longevity, especially if they should exceed those underlying the Alternative III projections, could also add to the anticipated funding problems of Social Security. Again, the case for governmental intervention rests on its greater flexibility in adapting to imperfectly forseen contingencies.

Social Safety Net. Not everyone will receive enough income in a market economy to maintain a minimal living standard. It is generally taken as axiomatic that our society will not countenance starvation or extreme deprivation among its less fortunate members. Private charities and individuals may assume some of the burden of providing for the destitute, but even libertarians like Hayek and Ferrara accept the necessity for a public program to guarantee that extreme needs will be met.[10]

A safety-net program would provide at a minimum sufficient income to cover basic necessities plus care for the medically indigent. Beneficiaries would include those who are unable to work because of old age or disability and those who are unable to afford medical care. If Social Security is eliminated, the welfare system would provide support for additional numbers of elderly and disabled. Public transfers would be limited to those truly in need. The remainder would be self-supporting through previous savings or previously purchased private insurance. Ferrara considers elimination of all public transfers except those that are means tested to be a major benefit of his phase-out plan.[11]

The availability of a public safety net for the indigent reintroduces the issue of moral hazard. A program such as supplemental security income (SSI) offers means-tested income maintenance for the elderly poor. Benefits are income-conditioned, and eligibility is subject to a wealth test. The existence of SSI weakens the incentive for individuals to save for retirement. Low-income households are most likely to be affected. Pressure to spend all current income on necessities is great, and the retirement income that could be generated by painfully accumulated savings may not be any greater than SSI benefits. More affluent households may also be affected. Some may exhibit a strong preference for present over future consumption (extreme shortsightedness); others may be encouraged to take exceptional risks in the market or at the racetrack or casino that leave them destitute.

Social Security forces individuals to participate in a program that collectively finances retirement. Would-be shirkers are not able to enjoy a free ride at the expense of their more prudent fellow citizens. Ferrara notes that shirkers can be dealt with by compulsory private savings. He also suggests means for limiting the problem within a voluntary framework. If benefits are kept low enough, welfare may be unattractive to all but the least affluent workers.[12] It might be added that forcing households with low earnings potential to save may not be good social policy. This is particularly true of households with children. The earned-income tax credit for low-income workers with dependent children indicates congressional concurrence. The credit provides what is effectively a partial rebate of Social Security taxes for such households.

Ferrara suggests a second step for combating shirkers. Welfare benefits could be available only to those elderly who are no longer able to work.[13] Experience with Social Security disability insurance (DI) undermines the practicality of this suggestion. The need to make such a determination for large numbers of elderly would be an administrative nightmare. Lack of suitable job opportunities for older workers, especially those with limited skills, would be a further drawback.

Ferrara's plan to replace DI with private disability insurance raises similar questions. If purchase is voluntary, less affluent workers will again be reluctant to pay the price when public welfare is available. Their reluctance would be strengthened if private insurers segment the market. Incidence of disability is higher among workers with low earnings. Insurers are likely to respond by charging higher premiums.[14]

Elimination of Medicare would require the elderly and long-term disabled to replace Social Security hospital insurance and the heavily subsidized supplementary health insurance with private medical insurance. Because these groups have the highest incidence of ill health in the population, the premiums for private insurance would be high. Since a public program for the medically indigent is a basic component of the social safety net, severe restrictions on eligibility would be required if shirkers are to be discouraged.

The likely ingredients of a means test for publicly financed medical care would include both a low income ceiling and a strict limit on wealth. Indeed, restrictions of this type are in effect for Medicaid.

If one believes, like Ferrara, that the elderly will be far more affluent under a private retirement scheme, the cost of medical care and insurance may be less of a hardship than it is today. Ferrara also speculates that in the absence of Medicare workers can begin making contributions to private medical insurance funds early in their working careers. By spreading the payment over several decades and allowing for investment fund balances, monthly costs could be kept at reasonable levels. Benefits would be payable after a specified age or at onset of disability.[15]

If private insurers could be induced to provide such coverage, and if individual workers could be persuaded to buy it, medical indigency among groups now covered by Social Security could be reduced. However, the incentive to forgo such purchases and to rely on the public program would not be eliminated.

Social Security as a Merit Good

The principle of consumer sovereignty is based on the tenet that individuals are rational and are the best judges of their own interests. Welfare economics is grounded on the principle of consumer sovereignty, and the theory of market failure applies to cases where markets fail to allocate resources in accordance with consumer preferences. The concept of merit good, in contrast, relates to circumstances where it is considered desirable to limit or overrule consumer sovereignty. The concept is a bit fuzzy, but according to one definition a merit good is one which, owing to imperfect knowledge, consumers will choose to consume in too small a quantity. In the case of merit goods the tenet that consumers are the best judge of their own interest is discarded, and an informed group may be justified in imposing its choices on those who are less well informed.[16]

Complexity, remoteness of benefits, and infrequency of purchase are among the characteristics associated with merit goods. Consumers frequently base decisions on information that is false or incomplete. In many instances, decisions based on imperfect information may have little impact on consumer welfare. Indeed, given the cost of acquiring information, a degree of ignorance is often quite rational.

In some cases, however, lack of knowledge may have serious consequences. In these instances, constraints on consumer sovereignty may be justified. For example, an informed individual or group may be empowered to act in the best interest of the individual, but how is "best interest" defined? One way is in terms of the role of agency. The role of an informed agent is to make a decision for an individual. Ideally, the decisions by the agent should be "perfect." Perfect agency requires the agent to make the same decision that the individual would have made if the individual had the same knowledge as the agent.

Perfect agency can be defined, but it is not an operational concept. The government often assumes the role of agency. Examples include compulsory school attendance, seat-belt laws, product safety regulations, and occupational safety. Private individuals may assume the role of agency, usually within limits set by government. Physicians prescribing drugs and treatment or mutual fund managers making portfolio selections are examples. Institutional constraints and agent incentives are likely to influence the agency role. Government employees are bound by regulations that interefere with efforts to accommodate needs of individuals. Private agents may be influenced by their own economic interest, which does not always coincide with the client's. Imperfect agents may, nevertheless, advance their client's welfare.

Retirement saving is frequently cited as a form of merit good. Decisions about saving, investment, and retirement are complex. Successful retirement planning must begin early. It requires the capacity to anticipate future wants, income streams, and family responsibilities. A proper investment strategy is required if wealth accumulation is to be adequate. Among the complications are periodic bouts of inflation, which require savers to choose between investments that protect the nominal value of principal and the generally riskier inflation hedges.

For generations economists have speculated that most people are "myopic," that is, that they tend to discount the future excessively. The charge is difficult to document directly, but evidence shows that most households fail to accumulate enough to forestall large drops in income at time of retirement. This phenomenon may be due to uncertainty over the effectiveness of saving. Episodes like the Great Depression or the inflation of the 1970s wiped out the purchasing power of previous savings and taught many savers a bitter lesson.

Remoteness of benefits may be another deterrent to saving for retirement. In the prime of life, thoughts of retirement seem unattractive. As one gets older and energy wanes, the prospect of working becomes more onerous. In other words, preferences change. Economists have formulated the life cycle model to explain lifetime allocation of work and saving. The model presumes stable preferences. If our preferences change, particularly with respect to attitudes toward work, we may find that we have locked ourselves into circumstances that we later regret. When we realize our error, it is too late to correct it.

Social Security does not relieve individuals of the need to plan for retirement or disability, but it does cushion earnings loss and ease reliance on prior saving and investment decisions. Defenders of the system find the government's role as an agent to be an attractive feature, worth the loss of autonomy that it entails.

Returns to Social Security versus Returns to Private Investments

A major appeal of a phase-out of Social Security is the presumption that private investments will yield higher returns to future generations than Social Security. The implicit rate of return in a mature pay-as-you-go system depends on the rate of growth of the payroll tax base. The relationship between rate of return and tax base can be stated precisely for a system with no reserves (hence no interest income), a given tax rate, and a constant ratio between years of work and years of retirement. Such a system yields a return equal to the sum of the rate of growth of the labor force and the rate of increase in wages.[17]

If wage increases are stated in real terms, the wage increase equals the rate of growth in labor productivity. Therefore, the rate of return is dependent both on demographics and economic performance.

Obviously, returns in a mature system are much lower than those enjoyed during the start-up phase. Ferrara and Lott (1985) calculated real returns for 1983 labor-force entrants. They range from − 1.5 percent to 2.75 percent, depending on lifetime income and family status. Projected returns range from − 1.5 percent to + 1.5 percent for all but low-income, one-earner couples.[18] If these calculations are correct, current entrants can look forward to real returns of about zero.

Others have estimated higher returns. Studies summarized by Aaron (1982) project real returns ranging from 2.5 to 4.0 percent for workers entering the labor force between 1960 and 2000.[19]

If, like Ferrara, one anticipates real returns of 6 percent or more on private savings and zero returns to Social Security contributions, Social Security appears to be a poor bargain for younger workers. The picture is even worse if savers could somehow capture the 12 percent before-tax return that he cites. On the other hand, when the 2.5 to 4.0 percent returns cited by Aaron are compared to the modest real returns of 3 or 4 percent on private pension portfolios reported in Bruno Stein's essay, a phase-out seems much less attractive.

We have no way of knowing whose projections are closer to the truth, nor can we be certain that historical returns to private investment portfolios will continue in the future. If the difference in returns is narrow (or nonexistent), the phase-out option will be unattractive to the cohorts that must bear the bulk of the cost.

Social Security Arithmetic

A pay-as-you-go social insurance system transfers income from working generations to the retired generation. The simple arithmetic examples that follow illustrate how windfall gains are enjoyed by the start-up generations and how windfall losses are inflicted on phase-out generations.

Phasing In and Phasing Out

Assume that each worker is employed for three periods (45 years) and collects retirement benefits for one period (15 years). Equal tax payments are spread across each working generation in each time period.[20]

Windfall Gains. A social insurance program is introduced at the beginning of period 4 when generation I retires, as illustrated in table 6–1. Since generation I paid no payroll tax, all benefits are in the form of a windfall. Each of the three working generations pays a tax of 10, yielding retirement benefits to generation I of 30. Since generation I paid no taxes during its worklife, it receives a net benefit windfall of 30. This may seem unrealistic, but recall that the first retirees under Social Security paid taxes for only three years and experienced very high rates of return on contributions.

Generation II pays into the program for one-third of its working life, pays taxes of 10, and draws total benefits of 30 for a net benefit of 20. Generation III is the last to experience a windfall gain. After paying taxes of 10 in periods 4 and 5, it draws 30 in benefits during period 6 for a net benefit of 10. Generation IV and all subsequent participants in a static, mature system will break even. This example illustrates why a pay-as-you-go retirement system is more appealing to start-up beneficiaries than to those who enter after the system is mature.[21]

Windfall Losses. Suppose that a decision is made to phase out a mature system. Again the impact of the system on six generations is illustrated, as shown in table 6–2. The decision is made to pay in full all benefit obligations earned through period 3. No benefit obligation is incurred thereafter, even though taxes are collected until the phase-out is complete at the end of period 6.

Generation I is the last to receive back in benefits an amount equal to previously paid payroll taxes. Generation II receives benefits of 20, which it earned for its period 2 and 3 tax payments. Since generation II must pay taxes in period 4 to finance benefit obligations to generation I, it experiences a lifetime windfall loss of 10. Because of the reduction in benefits paid to genera-

Table 6–1
Intergenerational Transfers during Phase-in of a Pay-As-You-Go Retirement Insurance Program

Generation	Tax per Period						Total Tax	Total Benefit	Net Benefit
	1	*2*	*3*	*4*	*5*	*6*			
I	0	0	0	—	—	—	0	30	30
II	—	0	0	10	—	—	10	30	20
III	—	—	0	10	10	—	20	30	10
IV	—	—	—	10	10	10	30	30	0
V	—	—	—	—	10	10			
VI	—	—	—	—	—	10			

Table 6–2
Intergenerational Transfers during Phase-out of a Pay-As-You-Go
Retirement Insurance Program

Generation	Tax per Period						Total Tax	Total Benefit	Net Benefit
	1	2	3	4	5	6			
I	10	10	10	—	—	—	30	30	0
II	—	10	10	10	—	—	30	20	–10
III	—	—	10	10	6 2/3	—	26 2/3	10	–16 2/3
IV	—	—	—	10	6 2/3	3 1/3	20	0	–20
V	—	—	—	—	6 2/3	3 1/3	10	0	–10
VI	—	—	—	—	—	3 1/3	3 1/3	0	– 3 1/3

tion II, during period 5 the liability of each of the three working generations, III, IV, and V, falls to 6 ⅔ during period 5. Generation III draws benefits of only 10, for a net loss of 20. During period 6 each working generation thus pays a tax of only 3 ⅓. All generations in the workforce during the phase-out are net losers. The biggest loser is generation IV, the new entrants during the initial period of the phase-out.

This simple example illustrates why a phase-out may not be attractive to young workers, even if they experience low or perhaps negative returns on their social insurance contributions. Ferrara, of course, is aware of this feature of a pay-as-you-go system. He is convinced that a supply-side boom will accompany the phase out, and that its proceeds will more than offset the unavoidable windfall loss. The phase-out will be self-financing and society will be free of a compulsory and oppressive system.

Supply-Side Effects of a Phase-out

Among economists much of the discussion over reform of Social Security centers on its effect on the supply of capital and labor. Martin Feldstein's alarming conclusion that Social Security has reduced personal saving in the United States by up to 50 percent touched off a new debate and stimulated much new empirical research. If pay-as-you-go Social Security significantly depresses saving and capital formation, a strong case can be made for a transition to a fully funded system. This could be achieved by transforming Social Security into a fully funded system or by phasing out Social Security and replacing it with individual retirement accounts and private pensions.

Social Security and Personal Saving: The Evidence

According to the life cycle model, individuals save for retirement during their working years. At retirement they replace lost earnings by drawing on savings or converting them to an annuity. In an economy in which earnings per worker or the number of workers increase over time, or both, savings or workers exceed dissavings of the retired. Retirement saving therefore generates a net flow of investment that enhances the capital stock.

Pay-as-you-go retirement insurance reduces the need to save for retirement. Contributions from workers are transferred to beneficiaries. The system's trust fund is very small relative to the flow through it, so there is no flow of net savings into the economy. Workers substitute Social Security wealth (the value of promised future benefits) for current saving, the asset-substitution effect. In this way Social Security depresses private saving and the capital stock, leading in turn to lower wages and lower per capita income.

This line of reasoning seems plausible, but it needs to be qualified. For example, if Social Security encourages earlier retirement, workers may increase retirement saving in anticipation of a longer period without earnings. We cannot predict a priori whether this phenomenon, known as the retirement effect, will be strong enough to offset the asset-substitution effect.

Other motives for saving exist and may be influenced by Social Security. Saving for contingencies, e.g., unemployment or major illness, may be affected. Saving for bequests might be increased, since older persons have less need to rely on personal wealth for their own maintenance. Indeed, increases in bequests could conceivably offset the intergenerational flows via Social Security. If other forms of saving are large relative to retirement saving, any reduction in the latter induced by Social Security will have only a limited effect on aggregate savings.

Resolution of the debate over the effect of Social Security on personal saving hinges ultimately on the interpretation of empirical results. The essay by Selig Lesnoy and Dean Leimer summarizes and evaluates a number of studies. These studies use time series data to estimate the value and significance of the coefficient of a Social Security wealth (SSW) variable in an aggregate consumption or saving function. Results of several earlier studies were compromised by use of Martin Feldstein's erroneous series on SSW. Lesnoy and Leimer reestimated many of the equations using a corrected series. They also report on more recent results, including their own extensive work which employs a variety of methods for perceiving and measuring SSW.

Lesnoy and Leimer found some SSW coefficients that are positive (Social Security reduces saving) but not significant; some that are negative (Social Security increases saving) but not significant; and a few that are negative, significant, but implausibly large.[22] They conclude that time-series evidence fails to support the proposition that Social Security has reduced private saving. The same conclusion can be drawn from cross-country comparisons and from household surveys.

Danziger, Haveman, and Plotnick (1981) seem to agree. After examining much of the same evidence, they conclude that Social Security has reduced personal saving in the United States from zero to a maximum of 20 percent with the most likely estimate at the lower end of the range.[23]

Social Security and the Retirement Decision

The labor force participation rate for men age 55 to 64 declined from 87 to 68 percent between 1960 and 1985. For men age 65 and older, rates declined from 33 to 16 percent. Rates for women remained stable, but this is because of the offsetting effects of the upward trend in participation and the trend toward early retirement. When participation rates of women age 55 to 64 are compared with rates for the same women at age 35 to 44, a pattern similar to that for men emerges. These trends coincide with several changes in Social Security, most notably the reduction in minimum retirement age for men to 62 and a marked increase in disability insurance applications and awards. The period was also marked by substantial increases in Social Security benefit levels and expansion of private pensions.

Benefit eligibility and the earnings test increase the opportunity cost of work for older workers. Some economists have concluded that after allowing for benefit reductions for early retirement, the present value of future benefits is maximized at age 62 for men. Consequently, they conclude that Social Security is the primary cause for the fall in labor market participation among able-bodied older workers.

If this is true, it has important implications for the economy and for the Social Security program. Aggregate labor supply is reduced, lowering the productive potential of the economy. Older workers are converted from Social Security contributors to beneficiaries, lowering the work-beneficiary level and putting stress on the trust fund, at least in the short run.[24]

Rachel Floersheim Boaz examined the evidence and concluded that demand factors, not retirement incentives in the Social Security benefit formula, are the most important cause of the falling participation rates of older workers. She cites evidence indicating that workers are less likely to choose early retirement if they have an opportunity to work full time at primary occupations. Both the level and growth of earnings play a role.

Studies that consider only the supply side are misleading. Demand for the services of older workers is equally important. Owning to lifetime earnings profiles and cost of fringe benefits (pension liability and health insurance) older workers may be costly to retain, especially if their productivity is declining. Consequently, some employers structure private pensions to encourage early withdrawal. Also, employment opportunities for older workers who lose their jobs are limited. For many, retirement becomes the only realistic alternative. Boaz concludes that the trend toward early labor market withdrawal is not likely to be halted and reversed without improvement in labor market conditions facing older workers.

Transition to a Private System

The cost of a phase-out to the initial working generation is seen as a major and perhaps insurmountable obstacle to radical change. These are the workers who will be forced to bear a large share of the cost, since they must finance benefits for their elders without promise of benefits for themselves. Two questions need to be answered. Do the potential gains from a phase-out exceed the cost? If so, how can some of the gains be used to compensate the generations that bear the cost? Ferrara poses the question this way: would subtracting the value of lost Social Security benefits from the overall benefits of reform make the phase-out unattractive to young workers? He concludes that it would not.[25] Ferrara concludes that income directed into private investments will yield a much higher return than Social Security. He quotes Feldstein's estimate of 12 percent or more before taxes. Much of the gain from this new investment will accrue to young workers. If the increment could be free of taxes, the full 12 percent could be realized directly. If not, the additional tax revenues could finance tax cuts or added public services. Either way individuals get the full return. By pooling risks in mutual funds, full, privately available, returns would be available to everyone.

Other sweeteners could be added to the package. Government could shift a part of the burden to future generations by borrowing to cover a portion of the cost of current benefit obligations, although Ferrara agrees that this would absorb a portion of the flow of incremental savings. In addition, young workers would be freed of the constraints imposed on them by Social Security. These include flexibility in planning for their own security, free choice of when to retire, and relief from worry over the impending collapse of Social Security.

Additional benefits include a stronger economy, more job opportunities, higher earnings, and a better entrepreneurial climate. As workers build up retirement accounts, the distribution of wealth would become more equal. Finally, the children of young workers would have a brighter future free of the tax liabilities of compulsory social insurance.

Are Ferrara's claims justified? No one knows for sure, but there are reasons for skepticism. Economic growth—the supply-side boom—is contingent on an increase in the savings rate. Ferrara is convinced that Social Security depresses saving. Therefore, a phase-out should increase saving. This may be true, but it is not supported by the evidence presented by Lesnoy and Leimer. We cannot predict with confidence that elimination of Social Security will have this affect.

A Closer Look at the Ferrara Proposal[26]

Ferrara's 1985 plan requires employees and employers to continue paying payroll taxes, since the revenue is needed to pay current benefits. Workers would be granted the option of contributing up to 20 percent of their OASI payroll tax liability to a "super IRA." Employees could direct their employers to make a similar contribution. IRA contributions would be offset by a 100 percent income tax credit to both employees and employers. Social Security benefits to workers choosing the IRA option would be cut proportionally. The option would be attractive to workers who expect a higher return from the IRA than from Social Security.[27]

The cost of the IRA would be borne by the Treasury, because the credit would reduce tax revenue. To make the credit option attractive to all workers it would be necessary to make a cash payment to workers whose income tax liability is less than their IRA contribution. The number affected could be quite large in light of increases in personal exemptions. One can only speculate on how employers with no offsetting tax liability would react.

As the phase-in continues, the IRA credit limit would increase, eventually to 100 percent of payroll tax liability. Credits up to 10 percent of OASI tax liability would be added to cover the purchase of life insurance. This feature would allow workers with dependents to provide them with protection against earnings loss as a replacement for survivors insurance.

By placing the cost of the super IRAs on the Treasury, some of the burden of the phase-out would be shifted from impacted workers to other age groups. If the cost is borne by higher income taxes, older Americans would share in the cost. In so far as revenue comes from capital income, the arrangement could lead to partially offsetting lower returns to IRA funds. Debt finance is another possibility. Distribution of the burden of debt finance depends on how the debt is managed. If the debt is financed by competing for loanable funds in financial markets (real debt), some of the burden could be shifted to future generations. However, this form of finance is competitive with direct private investment. If the debt is financed by monitization (disquised money creation) the result will be inflation, at least according to the conventional wisdom.

During the phase-in Ferrara would require workers to contribute to approved IRA retirement accounts or to remain in Social Security. If a large number opt for the super IRA, it is possible that aggregate saving will increase. Ferrara proposes that IRA contributions financed by the full income tax credit be locked in until age 58 ½. Thus super IRAs could not be readily substituted for other forms of saving. It is possible that workers will respond by saving more. It is also possible that they will reduce other forms of saving in an effort to maintain consumption. We do not know to what extent a fall in other forms of saving will offset the increase in retirement saving. Remember that the IRA contribution is not free; it is presumably financed by some form of tax.

In the long run, Ferrara predicts that Social Security, like the Marxist state, will whither away. Higher returns from private investments will cause more and more workers to opt for IRAs over Social Security. As successive generations become attuned to the private alternatives, mandatory retirement saving will no longer be necessary. An even more radical departure would be needed if government's role is to disappear completely. Ferrara's proposal does not at this point call for elimination of tax shelters or federal regulation of mutual funds and private pensions.

A Summing Up

The debate over Social Security is certain to be long and emotional. These essays deal primarily with the economic issues of factor supply and economic growth, income distribution, and market failure. All of these issues, especially those associated with distribution, have important political and philosophical dimensions as well. The debate over paternalism versus individualism is perhaps more philosophical than economic. Economists devised the merit-good concept as a means of approaching the issue, but many feel uncomfortable with this type of question.

Market failure is clearly present in markets for insurance. The presence of market failure gives economists a basis for recommending corrective intervention by government. But government, too, is imperfect, complicating our efforts to prescribe its proper role. To me, the most serious source of market failure in the area of economic security is that related to social risks. These risks are both economic and biological in nature. Inflation, depression, demographic cycles, and medical advances affecting longevity can put severe pressures on a system of social insurance. To private insurers these risks are generally uninsurable. Yet they exist, and they are likely to be a serious deterrent to efforts to engineer a phase-out within a generation or two.

Social Security is unquestionably coercive and paternalistic. It is also relatively inexpensive to administer, and it provides many less affluent beneficiaries with economic independence free of the regimentation of a means-tested welfare program. These issues should be debated, and they deserve careful consideration by the generation of younger workers who are most affected by the system's long-range problems.

The basic conclusion of these essays is that the gains from a phase-out are smaller than Ferrara claims they will be. Consequently, the risks are higher. If we reject his approach, however, we still must make difficult decisions about the future of the system. A crisis in Medicare is likely before the end of the century. The old age and survivors and disability insurance (OASDI) funds are expected to develop a large surplus over the next three decades, to be followed by fund depletion and, perhaps, another crisis. We do not know how Congress will react to these developments. Even if we reject a phase-out, we would be well advised to consider a phase-down. Ferrara's recent plan for a modest beginning provides a promising blueprint for less radical reform.

Notes

1. Public or social goods are characterized by nonrivalry in consumption, that is, where consumption by one individual does not reduce the benefits derived by others. Common textbook examples are national defense, flood control, and transmission of TV signals. If nonpayers can be excluded, private firms can supply a public good by charging an access fee, as with pay TV. Where exclusion is not feasible, as in the case of national defense, provision by government is usually required.

2. See Ferrara (1980), pp. 285–287 and Ferrara (1985a), pp. 91–92.

3. Heimer (1985) discusses the two types of moral hazard, noting that the economically rational variety is sometimes called "morale hazard." She describes various ways in which insurers deal with the two types of reaction. See Heimer (1985), pp. 28–48.

4. For a discussion of the effects of disability on labor force participation and earnings see Meyer (1979), pp. 21–31.

5. Some critics blame Medicare and Medicaid for causing the increase in cost of medical care. The issues are complex and controversial. For a survey of issues and results see Pauly (1986).

6. *Arizona Governing Committee* v. *Norris*.

7. Optimal product differentiation is of particular relevance in markets characterized by monopolistic competition. See Dixit and Stiglitz (1977).

8. See Ferrara (1980), pp. 149–150, 367–368.

9. See Hayek (1960), p. 295.

10. See Hayek (1960), pp. 285–286; Ferrara (1980), p. 364.

11. See Ferrara (1980), pp. 60, 363.

12. See Ferrara (1980), p. 364.

13. See Ferrara (1980), pp. 363–364.

14. Ferrara argues that private insurers will administer disability insurance more efficiently than the Social Security Administration. Private insurers will be more diligent in weeding out fakes and malingerers, since failure to do so will force them to raise premiums and lose customers. He seems to overlook the added cost of administering individual policies and of litigating questionable claims.

15. See Ferrara (1980), p. 362.

16. The merit-good concept was introduced into the modern literature by Musgrave (1959), pp. 13–14, although the underlying idea may be traced back at least to Pigou. For elaborations of Musgrave's analysis see Head (1962) and Pazner (1973).

17. The models on which this conclusion is based were developed by Samuelson (1958) and Aaron (1966).

18. Ferrara and Lott (1985), pp. 19–23. They based their projections on the alternative IIB intermediate assumptions in the 1983 Annual Report of the Board of Trustees of the Social Security Trust Funds.

19. Aaron (1982), pp. 73–75. Aaron also notes that estimates of negative present value of net Social Security benefits need not imply negative rates of return. The discrepancy can occur if the internal rate of return is less than the rate used to calculate discounted present value. See Aaron (1982), p. 75.

20. These assumptions would be satisfied if each generation is of equal size, all individuals die after four periods, and wages are constant. This situation is conceptually simple, but other more complicated relationships could yield the same result.

21. If the earnings base is growing, successive generations will receive positive net benefits even in a mature system. For an arithmetic example see Browning (1973).

22. The significant negative coefficients are implausible because they imply that aggregate savings would be negative in the absence of Social Security.

23. See Danziger, Haveman, and Plotnick (1981), p. 1006.

24. If the benefit reduction is actuarially sound, there should be no long-term effect on the fund. If the benefit reduction is actuarially insufficient for men, as some claim, there would be a net drain on the fund.

25. See Ferrara (1985b), p. 178. For a rigorous statement of the problem see Buchanan (1983). Ferrara's analysis is found in Ferrara (1985b).

26. Ferrara's 1985 plan is described in Ferrara (1985c). It is summarized in the introductory essay in this volume.

27. The various redistributive features in Social Security could influence this choice. This seems to be why Ferrara proposed in 1980 that these features, except for inflation protection, be eliminated. See Ferrara (1980), pp. 372–375.

Bibliography

Aaron, H.J. (1966). "The Social Insurance Paradox," *Canadian Journal of Economics and Political Science* (32), August, pp. 371–377.

———. (1982). *Economic Effects of Social Security* (Washington, DC: The Brookings Institution).

Browning, E.K. (1973). "Social Insurance and Intergenerational Transfers," *Journal of Law and Economics* (16), October, pp. 215–237.

Buchanan, J.M. (1983). "Social Security Survival: A Public-Choice Perspective," *Cato Journal* (3), Fall, pp. 339–353.

Danziger, S., R. Haveman, and R. Plotnick. (1981). "How Income Transfer Programs Affect Work, Savings, and the Income Distribution: A Critical Review," *Journal of Economic Literature* (19), September, pp. 975–1028.

Dixit, A.K. and J.E. Stiglitz. (1977). "Monopolistic Competition and Optimum Product Diversity," *American Economic Review* (67), June, pp. 297–308.

Ferrara, P.J. (1980). *Social Security: The Inherent Contradiction* (San Francisco, CA: Cato Institute).

———. (1985a). "The Political Foundations of Social Security," in P.J. Ferrara, ed., *Social Security: Prospects for Real Reform* (Washington, DC: Cato Institute), pp. 89–97.

———. (1985b). "Social Security Reform: Some Theoretical Observations," in P.J. Ferrara, ed., *Social Security: Prospects for Real Reform* (Washington, DC: Cato Institute), pp. 173–189.

———. (1985c). "Social Security and the Super IRA: A Populist Proposal," in P.J. Ferrara, ed., *Social Security: Prospects for Real Reform* (Washington, DC: Cato Institute), pp. 193–220.

——— and J.R. Lott, Jr. (1985). "Rates of Return Promised by Social Security to Today's Young Workers," in P.J. Ferrara, ed., *Social Security: Prospects for Real Reform* (Washington, DC: Cato Institute), pp. 13–32.

Hayek, F.A. (1960). *The Constitution of Liberty* (Chicago, IL: University of Chicago Press).

Head, J.G. (1966). "On Merit Goods," *Finanzarchiv* (25), January, pp. 1–29.

Heimer, C.A. (1985). *Reactive Risk and Rational Action* (Berkeley, CA: University of California Press).

Meyer, C.W. (1979). *Social Security Disability Insurance* (Washington, DC: American Enterprise Institute).

Musgrave, R.A. (1959). *The Theory of Public Finance* (New York, NY: McGraw-Hill Book Co.).

Pauly, M.V. (1986). "Taxation, Health Insurance, and Market Failure in the Medical Economy," *Journal of Economic Literature* (24), June, pp. 629–675.

Pazner, E.A. (1973). "Merit Wants and the Theory of Taxation," *Public Finance* (27), No. 4, pp. 460–472.

Index

About the Contributors

Rachel Floersheim Boaz, Ph.D., is a project director with the Center for Social Research, Graduate School and University Center, City University of New York. Her research focuses on the economic issues of maintaining the income and financing the health care of the older population.

Selig D. Lesnoy and **Dean R. Leimer** are economists with the Office of Research, Statistics, and International Policy, Social Security Administration, Washington, D.C. Their published research has had a major impact on the debate over the effect of Social Security on saving and investment.

Bruno Stein is a professor of economics and director of the Institute of Labor Relations at New York University. His publications include *Social Security and Pensions in Transition* and *On Relief: The Economics of Poverty and Public Welfare.* Dr. Stein's research interests include Social Security, labor markets, and incomes policy. He is a widely recognized authority on social insurance and private pensions.

Nancy L. Wolff is a NIMH postdoctoral fellow at the Center for Health Economics and Law, Department of Economics, University of Wisconsin-Madison. Her research interests include medical economics and economics of Social Security.

About the Editor

Charles W. Meyer is a professor of economics at Iowa State University. He is author of *Social Security Disability Insurance* and coauthor of *Principles of Public Finance*. He was visiting professor at the Institute for Research on Poverty at the University of Wisconsin-Madison in 1968–69 and was an economist at the Office of Research and Statistics, Social Security Administration, in 1973–74.

His research interests include social insurance, income maintenance, public choice, and the economics of taxation.